"Stop Raising Einstein *gives the reader the tools to embrace* ___ *themselves & others, and shows them that anything is possible when you believe in your dreams.*"
—MICHAEL ERUZIONE, Captain of the "Miracle on Ice" 1980 USA Gold Medal Hockey Team

"*Teaching your children to dream big and live their lives in pursuit of those dreams may be the greatest gift you could ever give to them.*"
—MICHAEL PORT, NY Times Bestselling author of *The Think Big Manifesto*

"*We are all blessed by the children in our lives. I have four. With each, my so-called 'parenting skills' were sometimes (probably too frequently) inadequate. In each, I learned as much as I taught, probably more. Through each, I grew as they grew. Because of each, I am a better person today. Tara's approach to affirming our children is not just a "guide for parents", but gives parenting purpose. Without purpose, shepherding our children through life can be motion without meaning or activity without direction. More than a century ago, psychologist and philosopher William James said, 'The best use of life is to spend it for something that outlasts it.' Spending our lives dreaming with our children rather than for our children will surely give them a richness to their journey that will remain indelibly etched in their hearts, a forever gift that will be an unparalleled legacy that will outlast anything else we could possibly do.*"
—BRIGADIER GENERAL RON SCONYERS (USAF, RET.), President and Chief Executive Officer, Physicians for Peace

"*It's never too soon or too late to dream.* Stop Raising Einstein *gives readers of all ages the tools and inspiration to find and live their dream life.*"
—MARCIA WIEDER, CEO/Founder, Dream University® and Author, *Making Your Dreams Come True*

"*A unique and interesting way for parents and children to experience excellence, life and growth together!*"
—CHRIS WIDENER, best-selling author of *The Angel Inside, The Art of Influence* and *Above All Else*, www.ChrisWidener.com

"This thought-provoking book has good news for busy parents who want to do right by their child. You can. It's called conversation and it's free. A much-needed message on how to strive for connection, not perfection. Read it and reap."

—SAM HORN, author of *Tongue Fu!® at School* and *What's Holding You Back?*

"Stop Raising Einstein is fun, powerful and inspiring! The writing and the exercises are engaging for both parents and children. If you want to make the next chapter of your life - and your child's life—the best chapter, take time to do it together—every week!"

—AMY JAFFE BARZACH, Co-Author of *Accidental Courage, Boundless Dreams,* President of Powerful Inspiration, Chair of Inclusive Fitness Coalition's Inclusive Play National Workgroup, National Advocate for Inclusion and Children with Disabilities, Founder and Director Emeritus of Boundless Playgrounds.

"Stop Raising Einstein is going to be such a gift to parents and children - really humanity. In her "real life" voice, Tara has made the mission of positive parenting and raising compassionate, self-actualized children accessible to all people. Any parent or guardian will easily be able to follow this guide and incorporate its teachings into their daily lives. Imagine what the world would be like if all children are able to do this kind of daily work with their parent or guardian. Our world would truly be heaven on earth!"

—HILLARY HAYDEN BURRI, Founder & President of Haydenburri Lane, Rascals & Routines and *Go Rascals!* childrens' book, toy and animation series

"Stop Raising Einstein lays the foundation for finding our "unique brilliance" and provides a message of hope for living the life of our dreams through the powers of focus, belief, and positive thinking."

—BRIAN A. MURRAY, MAJOR, USMC (RET), Vice President, Operations Marine Toys for Tots Foundation

"Tara …. This tool you've created is wonderful! As a Social Worker, restoring family relationships is key to family success. Your outline and suggestions for positive family time through journaling works very well. The process is explained well with easy reading and heartfelt examples. I use this tool daily to restore and maintain positive family communication. Your book creates opportunity for change, openness and fairness between members. I cannot say enough. Good job!"

—DELILAH A. REMP, Community Habilitation Specialist, JusticeWorks YouthCare

"Whether you are raising a family or raising your own life to the next level, Stop Raising Einstein *is a guide to embracing what is essential to each of our lives and to the world - freedom, generosity, integrity and love."*

—TOM TUOHY, President and Founder, Dreams for Kids, Author of *Kiss of a Dolphin*

Stop Raising Einstein

DISCOVER THE
UNIQUE BRILLIANCE IN **YOUR CHILD...**
AND YOU

Tara Kennedy-Kline

Published by Advantage, Charleston, South Carolina.
Member of Advantage Media Group.

ADVANTAGE is a registered trademark and the Advantage colophon is a trademark of Advantage Media Group, Inc.

Printed in the United States of America.

ISBN: 978-1-59932-151-6
LCCN: 2009937345

This publication is designed to provide accurate and authoritative information in regard to the subject matter covered. It is sold with the understanding that the publisher is not engaged in rendering legal, accounting, or other professional services. If legal advice or other expert assistance is required, the services of a competent professional person should be sought.

Most Advantage Media Group titles are available at special quantity discounts for bulk purchases for sales promotions, premiums, fundraising, and educational use. Special versions or book excerpts can also be created to fit specific needs.

For more information, please write: Special Markets, Advantage Media Group, P.O. Box 272, Charleston, SC 29402 or call 1.866.775.1696.

Visit us online at **advantagefamily**.com

Acknowledgements

It seems impossible to me that in living a life of finding the brilliance in every person, that I would even attempt to thank just a few. Every person I have ever met & every conversation I have ever had has lead to the person/mother/wife/ author and business owner I am today.

Ultimately, however, there would be no story if not for my Dad, Jeanne, Jillian & Becky, my amazing husband Chris and my greatest gifts…my boys Max & Alex! You are my inspiration and I love you!

My circle of excellence is not an Earthly one. In my deep thoughts and meditations on this project, I was guided by my Angels: Jesse, Uncle Bob, Steph, Greg, Nana & Pop Pop, Ken, Mammy & Pappy and of course, Mom. It was at these meetings I was able to learn and finally say Good-Bye.

To my Advantage Family—Thank you for your guidance, support, & unbelievable knowledge!

Sam Horn—You brought this idea out of my head and into the world. There aren't enough words to thank you for that gift.

Marcia Wieder, Tim Kelly, Jeffery VanDyke & Lynn Hargis~ You have no idea how you have saved me. My Dream Coach® friends are now family and I am blessed just for knowing you…But that was really the plan all along, wasn't it?

Faye—I hear you in my heart everyday. You believed in me above anyone else in my life and you put me center stage to show it. I love you.

Brian & Jana—You are my proof that Dreams do come true and Miracles can happen.

To my family, friends, teachers, coaches, fellow parents & Dreamers:

There isn't enough ink on the planet to thank you all for all you've done. You are each a gift to the world and I am a better person just for having known you.

Shine Brilliantly!

Table of Contents

8 *Preface*

11 *Prologue*

16 *About This Journal*

18 *Chapter 1:*
Just Listen to Me—Using Respectful Communication

32 *Chapter 2:*
Become the Coolest Person You Know— Lessons on Integrity

45 *Chapter 3:*
Make Life Easier— Setting Goals and Intentions

59 *Chapter 4:*
Learning to Fly— Finding Gifts in Our Mistakes

74 *Chapter 5:*
Make Life an Adventure— Live on Purpose

86 *Chapter 6:*
Flip the Switch— Focus on Gratitude

101 *Chapter 7:*
Dig Deep— When We Give We Receive

115 *Chapter 8:*
Leave Love Notes— Twenty-five Things I Love about You

128 *Chapter 9:*
See Beyond Your Beliefs — Live the Life You Dream

142 *Chapter 10:*
Surround Yourself with Light— Raising Your Attitude Average

153 *Chapter 11:*
Give Them a Dark Hall to Run Down — Creating Your Quiet Space

167 *Chapter 12:*
That Was Then, This Is Now — Resolve and Resolutions

178 *Afterword*

180 *About the Author*

"The ideals which have lighted my way, and time after time have given me new courage to face life cheerfully, have been Kindness, Beauty, and Truth.."

I MARRIED CHRIS, MY HIGH SCHOOL SWEETHEART, and have two exceptionally bright sons, Max and Alex.

At ten, Max is a boy's boy. An avid football and baseball player, he loves the great outdoors and is happiest playing with his buddies in our backyard. He plays the saxophone, and his most prized possession is his guinea pig, Hershey. His dream is to be a chef and someday own his own restaurant.

Alex is eight. He is a bundle of energy and is wicked smart, which can be somewhat overwhelming. He corrects Max's homework as well as his classmates', not to mention the grammar and whatnot of his teachers and his parents. He loves karate, soccer, and singing, and is great at telling jokes. He can build just about anything out of Lego's or mud, and he dreams of being an astronaut and building a rollercoaster on the moon.

My kids sound pretty great because they are. They also sound like two perfectly normal kids. They even look like two perfectly normal kids, but the fact is that my younger son is "on-the-spectrum." And in kindergarten, he was given what's called an IEP, which is his own personal reminder that he has Asperger's Syndrome.

Upon discovering his diagnosis and researching the symptoms, I thought, *Cool! A little aloof, but he's organized and brilliant.* The thing is, though people with Asperger's are often exceptionally gifted, they often also lack social skills, are prone to eccentric and repetitive behaviors, have a preoccupation with rituals, and suffer with communication issues. Alex exhibits a range of these symptoms; he is an amazing boy, but it hasn't always been easy to be a good mother, father or brother to him.

There is another boy who grew up with many of the same habits as Alex. He was a daydreamer, unfocused, loud, and aggressive. He liked to build things. He was socially awkward, quick to anger, didn't easily make or keep friends, and was considered a loner.

His name was Albert Einstein.

It is suspected that he may have had Asperger's Syndrome. Shocked? If you know a child on the spectrum, you're probably not. The thing that is most shocking to me is the realization that had Albert Einstein been a child today, considering what would have happened to that brilliant mind had he been diagnosed and "treated" for his disorder because his actions and behaviors didn't "fit in? What would the world be missing had he not been allowed to flourish in his own unique brilliance? As parents and caregivers of our children, we get to witness their uniqueness. We can see the gifts in their symptoms. We get to laugh at their silly, hour-long jokes and imagine what it will be like when they finally get to build the rollercoaster on the moon that they've been daydreaming about. At the end of the day we feel blessed to have been named supreme keeper of the secrets of our Einsteins. Kids are kids, and we hold the power to help make all their wishes and dreams come true, whether they are "on the spectrum" or not!

The goal of this book is not intended to cure children of what ails them. I am not a licensed physician or a counselor. I am simply a wife and mother who found herself at a crossroads. My husband and sons communicate differently; I found a way to meaningfully communicate with all of them. I guess you could say I chose to bend so they didn't break.

Around the same time as my son's diagnosis, I was diagnosed with depression and Attention Deficit Disorder. According to the professionals, I should be on Prozac and my son should be on Ritalin. Why? Because I get sad and he moves too much? Because I'm disorganized and he openly disagrees with some of my rules? Because I chose to focus on the negative instead of giving thanks for the gifts in life, and he hates bright lights and crowds? Seriously, that's called being unique and knowing when to cut back on the caffeine.

We all know that there's no handbook for parents. I like to consider this a trouble-shooting guide. My goal is that you and your family will begin to see the gifts in each other and develop a relationship of open communication, respect, and unconditional love. I begin each chapter with a few wise words from Einstein, and then move on to provide activities, journal prompts, and food for thought. Open your mind and heart to one another's dreams and imagine the possibilities! The fact is, each of us shines brilliantly in our own way and we are all raising unique little Einsteins.

Yours,

Tara Kennedy-Kline

"When the solution is simple, God is answering."

AT SOME POINT ALONG THE WAY of mothering a child with Asperger's, I figured out that I was sending my son away for seven hours a day so someone else could "fix" him when all I needed to do was play with him. I don't want to make it sound too simple, but a little play, a little understanding, a little journaling, and a lot of fun made all the difference.

It took me years to recognize this. It was a long road. I suffered from clinical depression, though I realize now that it was something I brought on myself. A number of years ago when my life spiraled out of control, I had two businesses severely in debt, I had just had my second child, and I was taking my kids to work with me every day. I was completely overwhelmed, trying to keep five plates spinning in the air at the same time.

It put a huge burden on my marriage. My husband found out about the debt while we were in the midst of refinancing our home. A necessary credit report unraveled all of the lies, deceit, and energy that I had spent trying to hide this fact. Everything was brought out into the open. Because Chris and I had different ways of looking at things, it didn't occur to me that we were on the same team.

That same year, I lost my brother, Jesse, to a heart attack. He was nineteen.

I carried on and went to counseling. They wanted to put me on medication. But I didn't understand why. I was mourning his death; I was *supposed* to be sad. I had lost my businesses and my baby brother; I was bound to have grief. At the same time, I was convinced that my husband was going to leave me and that he would take the kids; why wouldn't I cry?

A short time later, my mother was diagnosed with leukemia. I went through this entire process asking, "Why is all this happening to me?" Still, I thought: *There has to be something more homeopathic than antidepressants.*

Sadly, over a three-year period of ups and downs, I just kept compounding things onto myself. I kept adding one more thing to my plate. By this time, I did have a successful educational toy business, but when the heat was off, even for a few months, I kept focusing on all the horrible things that I thought were happening to me.

Then, Alex started full-day kindergarten. We always knew that something was up with him. We had tried to take him into preschool to socialize him. But where Max was a very jovial kid who would run in and greet his friends and be really happy to be there, Alex would curl up on the floor, cover his ears, and say, "Too many kids, Mom, too many kids." Transitions were a nightmare. When the other children would drop their crafts to line up for recess, Alex would throw a temper tantrum and destroy whatever he was working on and he would hide under the table when it was time to leave. If somebody didn't sit on the right rug square in circle time, he would beat the child up.

We absolutely knew that there was something unique about him, but we just couldn't put our finger on what it was. As time went by, he became more and more destructive. Mesmerized by fire, he would hunt down lighters or anything with a flame. He took a straight blade and cut through all the lines in our corduroy sofa cover. If we took him into a new environment, he would have a meltdown. If we took him to Max's wrestling matches, where there were bright lights and noise, he would rip away from us and run away down a dark hallway because it just flipped him out so much.

The thing that scared me the most was that we were leaving in a few months for Brazil and the boys were going with us. I kept thinking, *If this is the way he reacts to strange situations, what happens if he lets go and runs away from me in an airport or on a bus?* I started calling all the psychologists in Pennsylvania, but it was wintertime and all the psychiatrists were pretty booked up because of SAD (seasonal affective disorder) — basically, patients who can't handle our cold, grey winters.

No matter what, I was determined to take him to a psychologist because I knew there was something really wrong. Finally, I convinced one doctor that he would eventually hurt himself if he was not seen. After a few visits, she diagnosed him with Asperger's. It took a long time for my husband to accept it. It's a hard thing to hear about your child.

During my son's work with the psychologist, I found myself torn between his needs and the needs of the rest of our family. My mother, suffering with Leukemia, had taken a turn for the worse. I really wasn't able to pay as much attention to what was going on with Alex as I should have because I spent every day at the hospital with my mother, who was losing her battle. In November of 2006, she lost the fight. This was the most difficult event for me in my life so far. In fact, there was a time when I realized that my children were experiencing the same loss as I was and I seriously thought Alex might have some version of post-traumatic stress disorder, and the diagnoses was a mistake. But the school evaluated him, and by the time he started first grade, they had put him on an IEP (Independent Educational Program), which gives him special instructional, treatment, and discipline methods and started him with an occupational therapist.

During this period, I had begun reading some books that were recommended by colleagues at work. I had also attended a seminar in which the keynote speakers were journal keepers. Their philosophy was to keep a gratitude journal and write down ten things that one was grateful for every day. That simple process started me on a habit of daily journaling. I introduced it to my family, and it's become an important part of our routine. We started out journaling at bedtime, but now it's become commonplace at any part of the day. I can ask my husband or sons questions at any time because we have developed open communication. Sometimes they even ask *me* the questions.

We find it's easy to talk to each other now. Where we used to have an environment of yelling and butting heads, we are now able to "pick our battles" or avoid them completely. Alex is more able to maintain control and calm himself down in certain situations. And Max who at ten years old, is going through a lot of peer pressure situations is able to talk through those situations and come to his own solutions. Our sons have no fear of harsh punishment or judgment or criticism from us for things that they may be doing wrong or things that didn't go right or poor choices they made. We accept each other for who we are a lot more.

Chris comes to me with problems now, which is still kind of new, and I'm able to talk about my feelings, which is something that as a mother I never felt I could. I'm able to honor my own needs and myself, which makes me a better parent because my pitcher is full. I'm able to give my family more of what they need because I'm not constantly thinking, *When do I get my needs met?* I'm able to take charge, and in doing so, I'm teaching my family to take charge of their needs as well.

It's been a long road from there to here, and not all of it has been smooth or even scenic. But the journey was a necessary and valuable one and it has made me and my family who we are today. No, we aren't perfect and we still don't always make the right choices, but we have learned that we are perfectly unique and brilliant just as we are. We have also realized a few other things: That it's okay to be different, that we are a great team who loves and supports each other no matter what, that the seven hours my boys are away at school, are simply for learning and growing and that none of us need to be "fixed."

"The most beautiful thing we can experience is the mysterious. It is the source of all true art and science."

YOUR THOUGHTS ARE YOUR LINK to your dreams, your future, and your heart. When something like a thought or an idea feels important or powerful to you, write it down! Not everything will be a secret key to your future, but it is fun to look back and remind yourself what you were thinking and who you were at a different time in your life.

Journaling is an incredible way to communicate. It can be playful. You and your child might ask one another what sort of animals you'd want to become if given a choice, or where you'd wake up tomorrow for breakfast. Would it be in Paris or the Serengeti, or would it be on Mars?

Journaling doesn't have to mean writing for hours every night. As a matter of fact, it doesn't even really have to happen at night at all! Some of my best ideas have come to me in the morning or in the middle of the afternoon. Sometimes all I need to write before bed is my list of thanks and a quote that inspired me.

This particular journal is kind of like a training guide to help you and your child begin the process of independent daily journaling. At the start of each week, take some time to read through the lesson you will be working on. You can choose to journal in your own book first and then use your words to explain the lesson to your child and help them journal in their book or you may choose to explore each lesson together.

Either way is fine as long as you each remember to record your own thoughts in your own journal.

Though you will be learning some very specific tools for communication and living a life of purpose, you can also take the opportunity to write down things that just come up during your conversations. Follow the prompts each day and then let your imagination fly. Eventually, it will become a unique piece of work, just like you!

In the first chapter you will learn about respectful communication and dialogue. This will help you immensely in your work over the next twelve weeks. Although you will be learning new skills and topics, this is definitely one skill you should practice every day for the rest of your journey.

Once you and your child have begun to work together through this journal, you may find it to be one of the best tools you've ever found to build mutual respect and to prevent arguments, meltdowns, and misunderstandings.

Chapter 1

Just Listen to Me— Using Respectful Communication

"Laws alone can not secure freedom of expression; in order that every man present his views without penalty there must be spirit of tolerance in the entire population.."

TARA'S TRUTH #1:
Every child has an opinion and should be allowed to express it without fear of rejection or punishment.

THE TALKING STICK

Traditionally, the talking stick, a Native North American ceremonial item decorated with eagle feathers and crystals, was passed to a council member who wished to speak during a tribe's council meetings to ensure that a chief was not interrupted. Some tribes used a talking feather, others a peace pipe, a wampum belt, a sacred shell, or other designated objected. A similar concept is that of the "conch" used in the book *Lord of the Flies* by William Golding. The only person allowed to talk during meetings was the one holding the conch.

Nowadays this concept is still used by many groups, especially in groups who need help preventing discussions from degenerating into chaos. A talking stick ensures the right to speak—and the right to be heard.

I am a natural born talker. One of the big things about my family is that we all have very big voices and very strong opinions.

Over the course of a seminar I attended, I learned a technique to use when communicating with a man. This technique was based on the fact that men don't typically open up, so when you're talking to a man, after he says the last word say nothing and count to thirty in your head. It is almost guaranteed during that time that the quiet will become so uncomfortable he won't be able to stand it and will start talking again to break the silence. Once he stops again, start counting again.

It sounds simple enough—but for me, it seemed impossible. My husband could go on forever. He loved to hear himself talk, so I knew this would be torture. As it stood, I was constantly fighting to get the last word in, or any word in for that matter.

Still, I was intrigued and thought to myself, *This could be kind of funny.* So I decided to give it a try on my phone call home to my husband that night. The previous nights' calls had left me in tears because I got worked up over an argument or misunderstanding. But this night, when Chris finished talking, I started to count to thirty. I didn't say anything, and he laughed. I thought this was kind of cool. "What are you doing?" he asked. "Just listening," I said. He didn't know what to say. He started talking again, and again, when he finished I counted in my head to thirty. And he continued talking.

This went on for quite awhile. Eventually, new topics started to come up, opinions, emotions, and feelings I hadn't heard before. I had yet to say anything in this conversation, but I noticed quickly that his tone grew softer as he talked. Perhaps, he wasn't feeling like he had to defend himself? Not the usual "you did this" and "I hate that," which was our regular game. There was more "I feel this" and "I would appreciate that." It was amazing and truly inspiring. I realized there was something to this.

That weekend when I arrived home from the seminar, my family and I had our greeting and everything that we normally do when I return home. Per usual, it was a "tackle mom at the waist" reunion, but my older son was being belligerently pre-teeny. He didn't want to talk to me. On the other hand, my husband really wanted to talk to me, and for whatever reason, my little guy, Alex, got really upset. He ran upstairs to his room. So I went up to his room to talk.

I walked into his room to find out what was up, and he immediately went into meltdown mode. "You're the worst mother ever and I hate you" kind of stuff that at two would be tolerable, but coming from a seven-year-old just pissed me off. In the past, I would have probably barked at him something like, "How dare you be so nasty to me after I've been away from you for so long! It's not okay to treat me this way! You can stay here in your room until you calm down!" But instead of fueling the fire of his screaming and carrying on, the new, enlightened me had a better idea. I decided that instead of fighting with him, I would get quiet and get down on his level.

I actually sat down on the floor and just listened to him. I listened, and then I counted. After each outburst ended, I would say nothing and count in my head. Halfway through the rant, he looked at me and asked, "What are you doing?" I replied, as I had with Chris, "I'm listening to you." Alex started to giggle and then laugh; then he started yelling again but stopped. He asked, "Why are you listening to me?" I replied, "Why wouldn't I listen to you?" His shoulders dropped and his face lightened. "You're really listening to me?" Cautiously I asked, "Yes, Alex, why wouldn't I listen to you?" To which he replied, "Because no one ever listens to me."

My heart was broken.

That one statement started a whole different topic of conversation that we had never had before, and through talking to him I realized that Alex never really got to talk. He never really got to have his say.

I realized in a moment that all those years of screaming and temper tantrums were simply because little Alex—the smallest of our household of four, the baby, who was carried until he was fourteen months old, who still slept with me when my husband was out of town, and whom I still carried in from the car, my baby—was never, ever heard. The fact was that if my husband and I were having a conversation in our home, or just bantering back and forth, if either of the kids tried to interject something, we really wouldn't let them talk. We would usually stop them and say, "This is an adult conversation."

Alex had to yell the loudest to be the voice above the crowd. He didn't get to have an opinion, because babies don't. Normally, what he said was childish and immature, so his brother dismissed him; his brother's friends, who were often in and around the house, dismissed him. My husband and I had such *intellectual* discussions—who would do the dishes, laundry, drive the kids to school, what's for dinner—that we didn't have time to listen to our youngest son's opinion. So he began to yell and scream to be the voice heard above the crowd. It made sense.

At that point, our family made a dynamic shift. When Alex and I went downstairs, we called a family meeting. We'd never done that sort of thing. We explained to Chris and Max what Alex had said to me. It really hit home with them as well. It was a reality that we hadn't even thought of before. We agreed that we wouldn't interrupt; instead, we would take turns. Each of us agreed that to wait thirty seconds was a recipe for disaster and failure, but we would count to three. So it came to pass that now, when we're having a conversation with another person, no matter who it is, we count to three in our heads after the person says their last word before we say anything. We give each person equal time to talk.

It has made an unbelievable change in our family. It's actually become a sort of inside joke with us. My husband tells other people, "Well, it's kind of like the talking stick. Everybody gets a chance to talk, but we don't have a stick."

Some families do use a talking stick, and I think that could be kind of fun, but it would quickly become a joke for my guys. So instead, we set a deal, a man's pledge, and a scouts' honor—for I learned a long time ago that female ideals have little place in my house—we agreed with a handshake and a promise to count to three, take turns, respect each other's opinions, and allow one another to be heard.

We have been using this practice for over a year now. People that know us can't believe the difference in the way we talk to each other. It's actually become easier to be around my family! Alex doesn't yell much anymore, because if he starts to get fired up, we simply say to him, "Alex, you know I care about what you have to say, and you will have your turn. Hold onto your thoughts until I'm done and then I will hear you."

Sometimes, all it takes is simply to say, "Max is talking right now" or "Let me finish my thought, please." One of my favorite moments was hearing my seven-year-old son kindly ask his father to "Hold that thought, please" when Dad tried to interrupt a very important and detailed description of music class!

The thing that's kind of funny is that we had kind of gotten away from having conversations with other people because conversations had become so frustrating for us. In doing this—in just taking our time and counting to three and not interrupting people and not trying to interject our opinion and actually taking the time to listen to what the other person is saying—we found that we weren't planning our next defense or planning what we were going to say, but actually taking the time to listen to what the other person was saying. We heard each other more and we had no need to yell.

No matter how you slice it, if there is too much yelling going on, it's time to look at the person doing most of the yelling and listen to them.

DAILY JOURNALING

This week, take turns using respectful communication. Count to three in your head after someone's last word before you begin to speak.

As you journal each day, be sure to let each person completely finish his or her thought before you respond. If someone interrupts you, patiently remind them that "we do not interrupt" and ask them to allow you to finish your statement before they speak.

In the beginning, it may be necessary to remind them that they will have a turn to talk and you will listen to them until they are finished.

Also, be sure to make an agreement that there are no wrong answers and certainly no critique or correction of anyone's feelings. Then make a promise to follow through and hold up your end of the bargain.

To get the full value of joy, you must have someone
to divide it with. —MARK TWAIN

Day One: What was the best thing about my day?

_____

_____

_____

_____

_____

_____

_____

_____

_____

_____

_____

_____

_____

_____

_____

_____

_____

_____

You're blessed when you can show people how to cooperate instead of compete or fight. That's when you discover who you really are, and your place in God's family. —MATTHEW 5:19

Day Two: What was my greatest accomplishment today?

_____

_____

_____

_____

_____

_____

_____

_____

_____

_____

_____

_____

_____

_____

_____

_____

_____

_____

_____

_____

_____

Most of us would be upset if we were accused of being silly. But the word silly comes from the old English word selig and its literal definition is "to be blessed, happy, healthy and prosperous."

Day Three: What made me laugh today?

_____

_____

_____

_____

_____

_____

_____

_____

_____

_____

_____

_____

_____

_____

_____

_____

_____

_____

_____

_____

*Finish each day and be done with it. You have done what you could;
some blunders and absurdities have crept in; forget them as soon as
you can. Tomorrow is a new day; you shall begin it serenely and with
too high a spirit to be encumbered with your old nonsense. This day is
all that is good and fair. It is too dear, with its hopes and invitations,
to waste a moment on yesterdays.* —RALPH WALDO EMERSON

Day Four: What frustrated me today and how could I have made it better?

_____

_____

_____

_____

_____

_____

_____

_____

_____

_____

_____

_____

_____

_____

_____

Each of us will one day be judged by our standard of life, not by our standard of living; by our measure of giving, not by our measure of wealth; by our simple goodness, not by our seeming greatness. —WILLIAM A. WARD

Day Five: What would I never change about my life?

_____

_____

_____

_____

_____

_____

_____

_____

_____

_____

_____

_____

_____

_____

_____

_____

_____

_____

_____

_____

Do all the good you can, by all the means you can, in all the ways you can, in all the places you can, at all the times you can, to all the people you can, as long as you ever can. —JOHN WESLEY

Day Six: If I were superhero, I would _____.

_____

_____

_____

_____

_____

_____

_____

_____

_____

_____

_____

_____

_____

_____

_____

_____

_____

_____

_____

_____

_____

Seventh Day Success Story:

* What did I learn this week?

_____

_____

_____

_____

_____

** What were some really cool things that
happened when I practiced what I learned?*

_____

_____

_____

_____

_____

* What would I change?

_____

_____

_____

_____

* What would I never want to forget?

_____

_____

_____

_____

_____

Chapter 2

Become the Coolest Person You Know— Lessons on Integrity

"The pursuit of truth and beauty is a sphere of activity in which we can remain children all our lives.."

TARA'S TRUTH #2:
A child is responsible for how she or he reacts and the results that she or he creates.

FISHING FOR TRUCKS

I ntegrity is doing the right thing even when no one is watching. It is basically being able to recognize what it is that you believe in—and then standing up for it. It's a "say what you mean and mean what you say" kind of thing. If something doesn't feel right for you, or if you're doing something that isn't in alignment with who you are and where you're going, don't do it.

The reason that I felt this was such an important lesson for my children is because children are so easily swayed by the opinions and ideas of other children, and they're molded by the opinions of the adults around them. So in other words, our children aren't born having opinions about anything. Opinions are created by their environment, by what they hear, and what they see.

However, our children *are* acutely aware of what seems right to them, so I knew I didn't want to impose my views on my kids. I wanted them to come to their opinions on their own, but I also knew that would require me to be an exceptional role model. Simple things that we take for granted like telling a little white lie on the phone affect our children's sense of right and wrong; they hear it and they pick up on it. It pretty much tells them that it's okay.

I realized that in living a life of integrity myself, I was teaching my kids that if you truly believe in and stand for something, it's okay to express that and to stand true in it.

One of the best examples, which is coincidentally a really cool "mommy moment" for me, was when Max had several friends over who weren't very accepting people. Quite frankly, many of the areas around where we live are not very diverse, but in our house, we believe that everybody is the same and everyone is equal.

On this particular afternoon, one of the little boys visiting our house started going into a whole story about how he was against certain religions and ethnicities. I stopped him in his tracks because that's not something that we condone, but the thing that was so cool was that Max looked at him and said, "Dude, you really don't believe that." His exact words were, "That's so out of integrity for you, and I don't even know why you said that." He then proceeded to give him an example of a mutual friend who fits into one of those ethnicities this boy was claiming to be against.

At first the other kid looked at him like he was crazy. He had no idea where Max was coming from, but eventually he got it. We find this friend catching himself before he slips up at our home now. But that first conversation showed me that Max is willing to stand up for what he believes in and guide people that he cares about to follow their own beliefs and stand up for what they believe in, not just follow the status quo and say what they think is cool instead of what they know is right.

One of the most important skills in creating the life of your dreams is living a life of integrity. Integrity means something a little bit different to each person, but the biggest signs of integrity are trust, honor, accountability, and truth. I'll say it again: say what you mean, mean what you say, and, on that note, complete what you begin. If something isn't true to who you are and what you want to be, don't commit to it and don't start it.

It also means that you keep the promises you make to yourself and others. The little boy who cried wolf is a perfect example of a person without integrity. He made promises he didn't keep and failed to tell the truth; as a result it didn't take long for people to stop believing in him and ignore his cries for help. That little boy was taught a very important lesson in integrity!

Once you begin to live your life with integrity, you will find that life in general will become a whole lot easier for you and everyone you deal with. You won't struggle with difficult choices, because you will know what's right for you and others will know what to expect from you. Decisions will flow naturally, and you will feel good about the choices you make.

Integrity is a valuable trait, but it isn't perfect. Just because we live our lives telling the truth and following through, doesn't make us flawless. Having strong integrity does make it easier for us when we do make mistakes (and we will!) to take responsibility, ask forgiveness, and clean them up quicker and easier than if we tried to cover them up or blame them on someone or something else.

One of the first steps in creating a life of integrity is to realize that you are in total control of the results of your life. That's not to say you have superhuman powers and can control the actions of others, but it is saying that although we cannot control what happens to us, we completely control how we react to those things, thereby controlling how that situation will turn out in the end.

Alex, my youngest son, has a tendency to want to blame others for everything that happens to go wrong. The thing is, I too, have wrestled with this problem. I've always seemed to blame everyone else for the messes I've made. So, at some point, we were going through this lesson of "you have to take responsibility for your actions."

One afternoon, Alex learned a valuable lesson. The kids were outside playing. Alex wanted to take a truck outside that wasn't an outside truck. I said, "Alex, you know it's not an outside truck. You shouldn't take it outside." But he insisted. He took it out with him onto a bridge over a stream in our backyard. He was standing there with the truck running it back and forth on the rails of the bridge. Another little boy came up behind him and scared him. It was then that Alex dropped the truck into the stream.

The first thing he did was start screaming at the other child. "Why did you do that? You made my truck fall into the stream!" It started a big battle. Then it came inside. Alex tattled on the little boy, "Donovan made me drop my truck in the stream. It's all his fault." I asked, "Alex, who took the truck outside?" He replied, "Well I did, but it's still Donovan's fault because he scared me and he made me drop the truck." I said, "Alex, what if you hadn't taken the truck outside?" Alex insisted, "Well then, I wouldn't have been able to drop it in the stream, but Donovan scared me so it's all Donovan's fault."

We went through it a couple more times until I finally said, "Alex, look, here's the deal. You chose to take the truck outside. You knew that it wasn't an outside truck, so now we have two choices. We can stand here and argue about this and blame other people for what happened, or we can go get Daddy's magnet and go fishing for trucks."

That was that. In that moment, Alex the Blamer became Alex the Problem Solver.

Really, the trick is to become the coolest person you know. Keep the promises you make with yourself. We take so much time keeping the promises to other people that we neglect the ones we make to ourselves. If you believe what you say and are consistent, others may disagree with you, but they *will* trust you and respect you.

That is how we are meant to be with one another. I honor my sons and my husband by leading by example and by honoring myself and the promises I make not just to them, but perhaps more importantly, the ones I have made to myself.

DAILY JOURNALING

I know with all this talk of accountability and choices, it may sound as if we don't have rules or consequences and things are all neat and tidy for us. That couldn't be farther from the truth. As the parents of the house, my husband and I frequently have to "put our foot down" and say enough is enough. Lucky for me, I had an amazing teacher early on in motherhood. Her name is Lane Nemeth. She is the founder of the company I worked for called Discovery Toys and I had the good fortune to hear her speak at one of our conventions. One of the things she taught us was that children in general are not born vindictive. They do not set out to be naughty and break our rules. When things seem to be getting out of control, what is typically happening is that there are simply too many rules to keep track of or that we as parents make the rules impossible to follow because we change them too often!

So instead of a laundry list of "dos and don'ts" we have "Family Pillars." Three unbreakable standards that are followed not only by the children, but by every person in our house. These pillars do not merely define what we can and cannot do, but rather who we are. They speak of our integrity as a family.

Those pillars are simply: No Hurting, No Disrespect, and No Lying.

When you do your journaling this week, consider who it is you are "being" in those moments when you have to make a decision or a choice, and then write from that place.

*What you don't see with your eyes, don't witness
with your mouth.* —Jewish Proverb

Day One: What does integrity mean to me?

_____

_____

_____

_____

_____

_____

_____

_____

_____

_____

_____

_____

_____

_____

_____

_____

_____

_____

_____

_____

As I grow older, I pay less attention to what men say. I just watch what they do. —ANDREW CARNEGIE

Day Two: What was something I did or said today that made me feel proud?

_____

_____

_____

_____

_____

_____

_____

_____

_____

_____

_____

_____

_____

_____

_____

_____

_____

_____

_____

_____

_____

Be more concerned with your character than your reputation, because your character is what you really are, while your reputation is merely what others think you are. —JOHN WOODEN

Day Three: If someone were describing me, what would I want him or her to say?

Always imitate the behavior of the winner when you lose. —ANONYMOUS

Day Four: What challenge did I face today that I handled with integrity?

_____

_____

_____

_____

_____

_____

_____

_____

_____

_____

_____

_____

_____

_____

_____

_____

_____

_____

Values are like fingerprints. Nobody's are the same, but you leave 'em all over everything you do. —ELVIS PRESLEY

Day Five: What is something I believe in so strongly that I am a marble pillar and cannot be moved?

_____

_____

_____

_____

_____

_____

_____

_____

_____

_____

_____

_____

_____

_____

_____

_____

_____

_____

_____

_____

_____

Give whatever you are doing and whoever you are
with the gift of your attention. —JIM ROHN

Day Six: Describe traits that my family
members have that show integrity.

_____

_____

_____

_____

_____

_____

_____

_____

_____

_____

_____

_____

_____

_____

_____

_____

_____

_____

_____

Seventh Day Success Story:

* What did I learn this week?

_____

_____

_____

_____

_____

** What were some really cool things that
happened when I practiced what I learned?*

_____

_____

_____

_____

_____

* What would I change?

_____

_____

_____

_____

* What would I never want to forget?

_____

_____

_____

_____

_____

Chapter 3

Make Life Easier— Setting Goals and Intentions

*"There are only two ways to live your life.
One is as though nothing is a miracle. The other
is as though everything is a miracle."*

TARA'S TRUTH #3:
A parent's job is not to decide what our children
will become; it is to support and guide them as
they become what they are meant to be.

INTENTION: A GPS-DRIVEN LIFE

One of the biggest ways that I failed my husband and my children in the beginning was that I didn't set goals, and I didn't allow *them* to set goals. I said I wanted my children to be in karate and I put them in karate. I told them what subject they would report on for the science fair, and that's what we did. I said I'm going to quit my job and stay home with my boys without ever considering how that would affect my husband's goals and plans for our future.

I never allowed them to be part of that decision-making process. I said, "This is what's going to happen for you," instead of saying, "What do you think you need to do to make this happen?" I was creating a family that was 100-percent dependent upon me for every choice that they made. By doing that I put so much pressure on myself that I would stress out, which I would ultimately take out on them.

The most important thing that we can do for our kids is to teach them how to set and achieve goals for themselves. As adults, we forget that setting and achieving goals gives us so much to grow on.

What are we doing by never allowing our children to set and achieve goals? We're not allowing them the pride that comes along with accomplishment. We're never allowing them to feel that they've done something great, that they've achieved something they've set out to do.

It's like programming a GPS system. If you get in your car and just start driving without a destination in mind, you'll wind up driving aimlessly. You'll never reach your destination, and you'll never get anywhere.

Of course, there are a lot of other things that go along with success, but setting an intention means that you have a focus point. You know where you're going.

One of the hardest things for me after I lost my brother was realizing how few opportunities to spend time with him that I took advantage of. So when my mom was sick, I went to the hospital as often as I could to spend time with her. The frequency of my visits frustrated my husband. Without my vantage point, he didn't understand why I needed to spend so much time there. At one point I had to say to him, "Look, here's the deal. I need to be with my mom. I don't know how much more time I will have with her. I will never again predetermine how much time I will spend there. I will never again cut a visit short. This is time that I need to spend with her, period."

Once I made my intentions clear to him, we no longer had conflicts. He knew where I was coming from. He knew my expectations, and they weren't unclear whatsoever.

On the same note, it takes a wiser parent to avoid a battle with a child than it does to win one. Let me say that again: *It takes a wiser parent to* **avoid** *a battle with a child than it does to* **win** *one.*

It seems like every time my family would be getting ready to head out for an event, my kids would come to me and say, "Hey, can I go outside to play?" I would be so frustrated I'd say, "Yes, please go!" and I'd send them out the door. They would go out the door thinking, *Okay, Mom said we could go play.*

In the meantime, I'd be getting everything ready to go. By the time we were already ten minutes late, I'd be trying to round up my boys, who were nowhere to be found because I'd told them they could go outside to play. When I eventually found them, they were involved with something, playing with the neighbor or engrossed in a game. By that point I was angry, and I took it out on them, so we were all at each other. The real reason we were angry was because I hadn't set any intentions. I didn't say, "Yes, you can play, and I need you to be back in ten minutes so we can leave."

If I had set our intentions up right from the beginning, everyone would have been on the same page and there would be no need for an argument. The fight could have been avoided altogether. But the problem is that most of us assume people already know what we want. We assume they know what we're thinking—and when they don't, we get frustrated. When you look at it this way, it seems pretty unreasonable of us to assume others can read our minds.

Besides stating our intentions, there's a lot to be said for setting goals and being passionate about those goals. Even when your odds are five percent, if you're passionate about it, you can do it.

Where the intention and the goal setting really had an impact for my husband, my kids, and me was our morning routine. In the past, we constantly fought and argued each weekday morning. Everybody shoved food down their throats, trying to get a million things done before we ran out the door. Finally, at my wits' end, I asked my boys to make a list of the goals that they needed to meet in order to make getting out the door in the morning a pleasant experience.

Alex made a laundry list of twelve different things that he wanted to do like make his bed, clean his room, and take a shower. While these things were important on a certain level, they didn't make getting out the door in the morning any quicker. So we narrowed it down: "What are the *four* things that you must do just to get out the door in the morning?" It came down to getting dressed, brushing teeth and hair, eating breakfast, and remembering his book bag.

Those were the four things that were essential for walking out the door in the morning. In addition, he added to the bottom, "And have a really good day." We all found that setting manageable goals and writing those goals down on paper made our lives so much easier. Each person's intentions became clear.

It was especially awesome that we could go back and actually say which ones we hit, which ones we didn't, and which ones could we could care less about—and scratch those off the list so they weren't a burden to us next time.

Another kind of goal list that my family has is our "pie in the sky" goals, our dream goals. One study says that if you write something down, you're *two hundred* times more likely to achieve it, which is pretty cool.

I had my boys make a list of fifty goals of things they want to do in their lifetime. Max's list includes things on it like, "I want to own a husky and a German shepherd," and "I want to go hunting with my Uncle Jeff." The kinds of things on Alex's list are, "I want to be an astronaut," and "I want to make the Earth healthy." He has simple things on there, too, "I want to go back to Brazil." He also wants to go back to Disneyworld.

My list includes 101 goals. They include everything from having a summer home in Florida to having my living room finished, which, as of this writing has been completed! Yeah Chris!
Our home was flooded awhile back, and after eighteen months, we still hadn't finished the floor. Another is to be on stage with noted speaker Jack Canfield. There are big goals, and there are little goals. One of my goals was to hike the Appalachian Trail. I wrote it that way thinking I meant the whole thing, but last summer we vacationed in the Smokey Mountains and did a lot of hiking. I found out when we came home that part of a trail I hiked was actually on the Appalachian Trail. When I was flipping through my goal book, I noticed what I had written. I checked it off with a sigh. *Yep, I did that. I hiked the Appalachian Trail.* And not being a nature buff, that was a really good thing.

ACTIVITY: MY LIFETIME GOALS

"All things are possible if you believe…" —MARK 9:23

Make a list of fifty goals you want to achieve in your life. This list does not have to be completed now, or even this week. Goal lists are living, growing documents and will change and grow as you do! Take some time this week to relax and dream about some of the things you want to accomplish in your lifetime. As you think of new things, add them; and as you accomplish goals on your list, check them off! The greatest thing we can do for our health, happiness, and spirit is to set goals and go after them each day. The bonus is this: Once you have written something down, you have a 200-percent better chance of achieving it! So get started!

In my life, I want to:

Max's Goals:

> *Become a chef*
> *Own a restaurant*
> *Own a German shepherd and a husky*
> *Visit Italy*

Alex's Goals:

> *Be a spaceman*
> *See a spaceship (rocket)*
> *Visit Brazil*
> *Get married*

My Goals:

>*Visit all 50 states*
>
>*Write a book*
>
>*Meet Matt Lauer*
>
>*Cheer for my sons at their graduations*
>
>*Dance with my children at their weddings*

DAILY JOURNALING

This week is the perfect opportunity to address issues such as what we do, what we need to do, and what we can skip altogether. The lists that you and your child will create over the next few days will help you identify how you can make your lives easier. It allowed my family to eliminate unessential things that we were cramming into our morning routine. After we figured out what wasn't working, we were able to find a solution that did work.

You can't hit a homerun unless you step up to the plate. You can't catch a fish unless you put your line in the water. You can't reach your goals if you don't try. —KATHY SELIGMAN

Day One: What are the four things I will do tomorrow morning to prepare for my day?

The reason most people never reach their goals is that they don't define them, or ever seriously consider them as believable or achievable. Winners can tell you where they are going, what they plan to do along the way, and who will be sharing the adventure with them. —DENIS WAITLEY

Day Two: Make a list of the activities I must complete tomorrow.

_____

_____

_____

_____

_____

_____

_____

_____

_____

_____

_____

_____

_____

_____

_____

_____

_____

_____

_____

_____

The tragedy of life doesn't lie in not reaching your goal. The tragedy lies in having no goals to reach. —Benjamin Mays

Day Three: From yesterday's list, what didn't I accomplish, what would I move to the top of the list, and what could I have scratched?

_____

_____

_____

_____

_____

_____

_____

_____

_____

_____

_____

_____

_____

_____

_____

_____

_____

_____

_____

_____

_____

All of us perform better and more willingly when we know why we are doing what we have been told or asked to do. —ZIG ZIGLAR

Day Four: What are four things I intend to do tomorrow? For example: Get my homework done before dinner, play a game with my family, pick out six toys to donate to charity, take a bath.

When we are motivated by goals that have deep meaning, by dreams that need completion, by pure love that needs expressing, then we truly live life. —GREG ANDERSON

Day Five: Today, I completed _____ of my four goals. How did that make me feel?

_____

_____

_____

_____

_____

_____

_____

_____

_____

_____

_____

_____

_____

_____

_____

_____

_____

_____

So when you are listening to somebody, completely, attentively, then you are listening not only to the words, but also to the feeling of what is being conveyed, to the whole of it, not part of it. —J. KRISHNAMURTI

Day Six: What was something that went wrong today as a result of not being clear about my intentions? How would I do that over if I could?

_____

_____

_____

_____

_____

_____

_____

_____

_____

_____

_____

_____

_____

_____

_____

_____

_____

_____

_____

Seventh Day Success Story:

* *What did I learn this week?*

_____

_____

_____

_____

_____

* *What were some really cool things that*
happened when I practiced what I learned?

_____

_____

_____

_____

_____

* *What would I change?*

_____

_____

_____

_____

* *What would I never want to forget?*

_____

_____

_____

_____

_____

Chapter 4

Learning to Fly— Finding Gifts in Our Mistakes

"Anyone who has never made a mistake has never tried anything new."

TARA'S TRUTH #4:
A child must be allowed to make mistakes or even fail
and suffer the consequences in order to grow.

MAX KLINE HITS THE BALL

Everything happens for a reason, so finding the gifts in our mistakes is important. I believe there are no accidents. Not everybody subscribes to this, and that's okay, but I believe if children are never allowed to make mistakes then they never really learn. Some of the biggest mistakes we make in our lives hold the biggest lessons.

When my business failed, I realized that I don't have to take everything on myself. If I'm not good at something it's okay to ask someone for help. First of all, I never would have gotten into debt if I had just realized that there are other people who are really good at accounting and business finances. I was so bound and determined to do it all on my own that I allowed myself to fail miserably rather than ask for what I needed.

I think that's another big lesson we don't allow our children to learn; by never allowing them to make mistakes, we don't allow them to understand that it's okay to ask for help. If we're constantly cleaning up the mess before they even make it, they never learn how to fend for themselves. They never learn how to be in a situation where they need to ask for help.

I also learned a very big lesson about how my assumptions led me down the wrong path. I assumed that everything would end if my husband knew about this debt. The worst possible case scenario was running through my head. *He'll leave me, he'll take the kids, and he'll never forgive me!* I allowed myself to go there in my own head, but the reality is leaving me was never even an option for him! When it finally came out in the open, I realized that he was my biggest advocate. He was the person who said, "Yeah, this is bad, but we can fix it. Let's fix it. Let's do this together."

Sometimes the lessons are subtle or we are so blinded by our own self-deprecation that we have a hard time seeing what we learned from them. When I was growing up, my dad had a sports events promotions business. One year, he held one of the biggest running races in the United States; world-class athletes came to this event because it was a qualifier for the Olympics that year. One woman finished the race in record-breaking time, which qualified her for the Olympic trials.

The day after the race, we got a call from a committee whose job was to certify courses to make sure everything was right. My dad told them, "We did have to make a last minute change to the course, but it actually made it longer, so that made her time even better," Unfortunately, their response was, "No, it actually disqualifies her because you made a change to the course without re-certifying it with us. You had sent us specific numbers and statistics. By making that change and not telling anybody, it disqualifies her."

That was a pretty big "oops" and we all heard about it for a long time, but I found out recently that over twenty years later, my dad has still been beating himself over this. When I asked him, "What do you think the lesson is, Dad?" he said, "I don't know." It was just so disappointing. We talked about this for quite awhile and eventually discovered the take-away is: That event made everyone involved more aware of how important our roles are in everything we do. My dad has actually become a stickler for detail, which is absolutely necessary in his current business. But what he also failed to see is that it made him better at his events business, too. From the day after that mistake, he became the best course certifier around. If you needed a great racecourse, you either used one of Dave Kennedy's, or you had him come out and certify yours. He would walk an entire marathon course pushing a measuring wheel if he had to just to be absolutely sure. Unfortunately, he was so blinded by his own guilt that he never allowed himself to see how much he was appreciated.

As for the runner, she did, in fact, qualify later on that year, and you can be sure she never again left something that important to chance.

The thing is, if we never learn anything from our mistakes then all we get out of them is something to beat ourselves up with for the rest of our lives. However, if we allow ourselves to go back and reflect on the mistakes we've made and see how they have changed us to make us better or more educated or wiser or more sensitive people as a result of those mistakes, then it helps us to understand that mistakes really do happen for a reason.

This is what helps each of us learn to fly. Every mistake and every failure that I can think of in my life has caused me to improve myself the next time. Maybe it caused me to think in a different direction or maybe it's like the old adage, measure twice, cut once. Without doubt, you will have to screw up a few times before you believe that.

One of my favorite stories relating to this is Thomas Edison's experience while inventing the light bulb. He made a ridiculous number of attempts, something like ten thousand, to make it work. When interviewed about his invention he said, "I didn't fail ten thousand times. I just found ten thousand ways it wouldn't work."

If we look at our mistakes in that way, we're not failing, we're becoming stronger. However, when we allow ourselves to constantly relive the mistakes that we've made in our lives, we bring more of that blundering activity into our lives.

Max has been an awesome batter since the day he started playing baseball. But one time at bat, the ball hit him. Several times right after that, he struck out. Soon, he started saying to himself, "I can't hit the ball." From that moment on, Max stopped hitting the ball.

We went through an entire baseball season where it seemed like Max struck out every time he was at bat. I asked him, "Max, you remember when you used to hit the ball?" "Yeah, I remember," he said glumly. I responded, "I need you to picture that in your mind. How did that feel? Watch the ball after you hit it. See that in your mind. I want you to make an affirmation. I want you to write down what it feels like to hit the ball."

His affirmation was really simple: "Max Kline hits the ball." Now when he goes to a game, if he looks like he's getting stressed out, or if he's swinging and missing, I can say to him, "Max Kline hits the ball" from the bleachers, which helps snap him back into a positive mindset. Afterwards people have come up to me and said, "What did you feed that kid?" because it takes him to a totally different place.

We are in control of our thoughts, beliefs, and actions. As a result, we are in control of our reactions (good or bad), and therefore we determine our results. It's kind of like a coach reviewing the playback with his team, pointing out were they went wrong, and then brainstorming to figure out how to do it better the next time.

Every person on the planet makes mistakes. Life is messy, but that's the point. The true secret is to find the beauty in the blunder. What keeps us from hitting the ball today—whether it is a mental block or an honest-to-goodness mistake—is what will eventually lead us to hit one out of the park.

ACTIVITY: AFFIRMATION CARDS

"I'm good enough. I'm smart enough, and doggone it, people like me!" —Stuart Smalley

Create a slogan for yourself.

Remember Stuart Smalley standing in front of the mirror spouting those passionate compliments to himself?

That was the start of a wonderful affirmation. My kids call them slogans, but that's okay, too. I actually kind of like that term—"a slogan for myself." That works!

I have many affirmations/slogans that I regularly say to myself and that always serve me well. As a matter of fact, it was an affirmation that saved me many years ago when I was at my lowest point in life.

One of my favorite slogans for me is: "Wherever you go, whatever you do, luck and success go along with you."

I know it sounds a bit cliché, but it was printed on a mug I received as a gift back in 1992, and it has served me well to say it out loud ever since!

Max has found his success with slogans, and anyone on the baseball team can tell you that it works. "Max Kline hits the ball!"

Alex, though he has a quick wit, he also has a sharp tongue. There are times when reacting in anger has gotten him in a lot of trouble. The upside is that he has developed the skill of attention and focus through martial arts. Using the two skills together, he has created the affirmation: "I stop and take a breath before I react."

The whole point behind affirmations or slogans is simply to help us "keep our eyes on the prize" to move us closer to our goals, and to give us a tool to "flip the switch" when we start to lose focus or faith.

So today, we're going to create a slogan (or three) especially for you! To get started, write down the following thoughts.

* Something you want or desire. For instance: "A healthy, 125-pound body."

* Next, write an emotion. It's good to attach a positive emotion to your slogan. Emotions make things powerful. For example: "I am *happily* looking at my healthy, 125-pound body in the mirror."

* A limiting belief or negative thought you carry about yourself in its opposite form. For example: "I cannot do math," would be written as: "I complete my math homework with ease and joy."

Things to remember:

> Keep negative phrases out. In other words, don't repeat what you don't want over and over again.

> Make it all about you. You can't make things happen for others, only yourself. (Do this simply by adding the words *I, me,* or your name.)

> Keep it simple! "I spread joy and inspiration wherever I go." "I handle every situation with love and patience." "I am thrilled to be at my healthy, sexy goal weight of 125." "I love my family. I love my family."

> Whatever works for you...

Now write your slogan on a card or piece of paper and read it out loud.

Have fun with your slogans. They're meant to bring love and more of what you want into your life—and isn't that worth shouting and repeating as a mantra?

DAILY JOURNALING

Each night I ask my kids what went wrong that they might have done differently. It gives them a chance to not only reflect and embrace anything that fate might have thrown their way, but also to figure out what they might do differently next time. They have a chance to own up to their mistakes while also understanding what they need to change. My sons like to imagine putting a problem they don't have control over into a bubble and blowing it away.

This week, when you write in your journal, think of something you did or something that happened each day that made you unhappy with the results. Then journal how you could have done it differently to get the results you would be happy with. Don't focus on the mistakes; they are in the past and cannot be changed. The future and the lessons are your gifts! Make them as bright and beautiful as you dream them to be.

Many of life's failures are people who did not realize how close they were to success when they gave up. —THOMAS EDISON

Day One: What is something that happened today that I would change if I could?

_____

_____

_____

_____

_____

_____

_____

_____

_____

_____

_____

_____

_____

_____

_____

_____

_____

_____

_____

_____

Forgiveness is the answer to the child's dream of a miracle by which what is broken is made whole again, what is soiled is again made clean. —DAG HAMMARSKJOLD

Day Two: What is something that upset me that I have not let go of?

_____

_____

_____

_____

_____

_____

_____

_____

_____

_____

_____

_____

_____

_____

_____

_____

_____

_____

_____

Success is failure turned inside out. The silver lining of the clouds of doubt. And you never can tell how close you are, it may be near when it seems so far. So stick to the fight when you're hardest hit. It's when things seem worst that you must not quit. —LILLIAN WHITING

Day Three: What is something that happened today that I must either clean up or put in a bubble, and blow away? What will I do and why?

_____

_____

_____

_____

_____

_____

_____

_____

_____

_____

_____

_____

_____

_____

_____

_____

_____

_____

Constant effort and frequent mistakes are the stepping-stones to genius. —ELBERT HUBBARD

**Day Four: One of my biggest mistakes was
_____. It taught me _____.**

Obstacles don't have to stop you. If you run into a wall, don't turn around and give up. Figure out how to climb it, go through it, or work around it. —MICHAEL JORDAN

Day Five: If I could change two things about myself, what would they be?

Before ending your journaling today, eliminate any negative thoughts by writing them as if they are positive and true for you. For example: "I am not good at math" becomes "I am good at everything when I give my best effort."

_____

_____

_____

_____

_____

_____

_____

_____

_____

_____

_____

_____

_____

_____

_____

_____

Use what talents you possess: the woods would be very silent if no birds sang there except those that sang best. —HENRY VAN DYKE

Day Six: What am I really good at?

_____

_____

_____

_____

_____

_____

_____

_____

_____

_____

_____

_____

_____

_____

_____

_____

_____

_____

_____

Seventh Day Success Story:

* *What did I learn this week?*

_____

_____

_____

_____

_____

* *What were some really cool things that
happened when I practiced what I learned?*

_____

_____

_____

_____

_____

* *What would I change?*

_____

_____

_____

_____

* *What would I never want to forget?*

_____

_____

_____

_____

_____

Chapter 5

Make Life an Adventure—
Live on Purpose

"Imagination is more important than knowledge."

TARA'S TRUTH #5:
As parents, we must show children that sometimes it's okay to
blur and even cross the lines between dreams and responsibility.

BREAKING THE RULES—LIVING THE
DREAM—OBLIGATION VERSUS PASSION

I believe that every person on earth has a purpose, and I believe that this purpose is within us from the time we arrive here. I call it a gift. However, I also believe that we're not ready to know it when we're born because as we live our lives and overcome obstacles, we're being taught the tools and lessons we need to eventually truly live our life's purpose.

I believe our purpose when we're born is to be innocent and to spread love and happiness. And that our purpose changes throughout life. I don't expect children to know what that is, but what I've found in my own search for purpose is that the things I've experienced and the feelings I've had throughout my life have really been tied to my life's purpose.

Because of these beliefs, it may seem odd that I would even touch on the subject of purpose with a child, but I'm hoping that as a result you and your child will journal about those things that you are most passionate about now. This will enable you to make choices and see patterns that guide you toward your purpose when you are ready.

What I think is kind of cool about doing purpose-hunting exercises with kids is that while you're both finding out those things that you love and that bring joy, energy, and passion into your life, you are also discovering hints and clues to what your purpose is. How amazing will it be in ten years to go back and look at these journals, see those things, and say, "Oh my gosh, I knew it back then. I was on the path to my purpose and I didn't even realize it."

As adults we spend so much time and money seeking out professionals to help us to find our purpose, and what these professionals are doing is simply taking us back to our childhood. How much couch money would be saved if we just started doing it now and kept track of it?

Sometimes we feel that we've gotten off course. It's because we have taken away our own permission to do the things we love in life. We focus so much on our obligations that we've started to ignore our passions. We put so much on ourselves, things that we consider obligations but that are actually impositions we make on ourselves. A big part of living your life "on purpose" is to bring more of what you love into your life. If you spend so much time fulfilling obligations to others that you neglect to do the things that you're passionate about and that bring you joy, you're not serving yourself. You're not serving your family. You're not doing anybody any favors.

However, when we bring more fun and adventure into our lives, we allow ourselves to experience life through our children again, and that creates an incredible bond and a mutual respect. If we allow ourselves to have more fun with our kids, we will gain our children's respect so much more than if we try to demand it. If we *earn* it, it's so much more powerful.

When I learned to play with my kids, it made my life so much easier and so much more fun. It helped my own purpose-hunting. It made it a lot easier for me because I was able to follow my energy and do what I love. This could mean trying a new food or making a new dinner. Play a board game together. Skip the meeting and order pizza. Have a movie night. Anything you do that's different from what you always do, anything that kind of mixes it up a little, changes the status quo in your house.

I don't know what my son will be when he grows up, but I can tell you that today, Max wants to be a chef. He wants to own his own restaurant and he already has a name for it (I'd tell you, but then he'd never speak to me again.)

Max's love of cooking and experimenting with food started while we were on vacation in Brazil. My children, like most kids, are on a four foods diet: peanut butter and jelly, chicken nuggets, mac-n-cheese and spaghetti. If it doesn't fit that menu, they will voluntarily starve themselves. This concerned me greatly since we would be in a very foreign country with very foreign food for nearly ten days. So, because my children love money and games almost as much as mac-n-cheese, I decided to make up an eating game.

On the first day at breakfast we began the "weird food of the day contest." Whoever ate the strangest food of the day got the unbelievable prize of five dollars. Alex tried to take the prize right off the bat by eating papaya off the breakfast buffet, but he was quickly out-done by dad who had some kind of smoked fish.

Over the course of the trip, we proceeded to consume a number of amazing and disgusting delights. There was raw coconut jelly, chicken livers, some weird sausage thing, an odd purple fruit called acai and, of course, my winning entry, spiny black sea urchin (I hate to be outdone). The boys ate things that I never imagined they would even allow to touch their plates. At the end of the trip, we all had a new perspective on trying new foods and Max had an overwhelming passion for kickin' it up in the kitchen.

We could have gone the route of some of our friends on that trip and stuck to chain restaurants and packing kiddy lunches, but that would have been boring and safe and in the long run, we would have missed an amazing experience with our boys. What we gained was invaluable and irreplaceable. We may just have inspired the next Iron Chef! Look out Bobby Flay!

I know not everyone can hop a plane to follow their passion, but who needs to? There are some things you can easily do around your house to mix up your routine. Simply rearrange your furniture. Do a brainteaser or a puzzle together. Order something different from the menu. Go on a hike. Play hide and seek or take a ride down the sliding board at your local park. You can do something goofy that you think your kids have way outgrown. You will be amazed at how much fun they have with it.

DAILY JOURNALING

One of the greatest memories that I have is of my mom taking me out of school for the day just so that we could go shopping together. I'm not condoning playing hooky, but everyone needs a "snow day" every once in awhile. With that in mind, we can teach our children volumes about how to honor one's self and one's passions by modeling the simple things, like to skip the PTA meeting and head to the playground. To make the choice to pick dandelions and eat peanut butter sandwiches rather than weed the garden and slave in the kitchen, or make sheet forts in the den rather than fold the laundry.

While journaling this week, let your whimsical side come put to play and answer your questions with the spirit and inquisitiveness of a child. When it comes to living on purpose—make life an adventure.

The person born with a talent they are meant to use will find their greatest happiness in using it. —JOHANN WOLFGANG VON GOETHE

Day One: The times I have felt the happiest in my life were _____.

_____

_____

_____

_____

_____

_____

_____

_____

_____

_____

_____

_____

_____

_____

_____

_____

_____

_____

_____

Adults are always asking little kids what they want to be when they grow up because they're looking for ideas. —PAULA POUNDSTONE

Day Two: If I could do one thing all day long, what would it be?

A span of life is nothing. But the man or woman who lives that span, they are something. They can fill that tiny span with meaning, so its quality is immeasurable, though its quantity may be insignificant. —CHAIM POTOK

Day Three: I think my greatest gifts are _____.

_____

_____

_____

_____

_____

_____

_____

_____

_____

_____

_____

_____

_____

_____

_____

_____

_____

_____

_____

_____

We all need a daily checkup from the neck up to avoid stinkin' thinkin' which ultimately leads to hardening of the attitudes. —ZIG ZIGLAR

Day Four: Others tell me my greatest gifts are _____.

_____

_____

_____

_____

_____

_____

_____

_____

_____

_____

_____

_____

_____

_____

_____

_____

_____

_____

_____

_____

Sometimes in our attempt to give our children what we did not have, we forget to give our children what we did have. —CONNIE PODESTA

Day Five: What are the top ten ways to show me that you love me?

_____

_____

_____

_____

_____

_____

_____

_____

_____

_____

_____

_____

_____

_____

_____

_____

_____

_____

_____

*A friend is a person with whom I may be sincere. Before him
I may think aloud.* —RALPH WALDO EMERSON

Day Six: What are the seven things I would like to do with a friend?

_____

_____

_____

_____

_____

_____

_____

_____

_____

_____

_____

_____

_____

_____

_____

_____

_____

_____

_____

_____

_____

_____

Seventh Day Success Story:

* What did I learn this week?

_____

_____

_____

_____

_____

* What were some really cool things that happened when I practiced what I learned?

_____

_____

_____

_____

_____

* What would I change?

_____

_____

_____

_____

* What would I never want to forget?

_____

_____

_____

_____

_____

Chapter 6

Flip the Switch— Focus on Gratitude

"To know is nothing at all; to imagine is everything."

TARA'S TRUTH #6:

As parents, we need to teach our children to recognize and to be grateful for the gifts they receive, even if those gifts don't come from us.

PUNCH BUGGY—NO PUNCH-BACKS

No one likes to give a gift to an ungrateful person. Neither does the universe. As parents we need to teach our children to be grateful for the gifts they receive.

One of the first lessons I learned about journaling was to keep a gratitude journal and every day write down ten things that I was grateful for. I was at a place in my life where I didn't think I was grateful for a lot, so I didn't think I'd have a whole lot to write on this subject. Ironically, when I started writing, I realized that I had so much to be grateful for that I was taking for granted. Things like my sight, the fact that I had a home, the fact that I could go to bed with a full belly. Those are all things to be grateful for. Once I started to journal with my children, I realized that as I taught them to be grateful for the simple things in life, they became overjoyed with the great things in life.

That to me was such a powerful lesson because there are so many kids today who are never expected to be grateful, and they grow up not knowing how to be thankful for anything. But our children have the capacity to be very thankful and very gracious if we give them the opportunity and the skills to realize it. I believe that we get what we focus on. If we focus on the bad stuff, we get more of the bad stuff. If we focus on the good stuff, then we get more of the good.

There are a lot of different ways to put this. Some people say that we're like human magnets and we draw to us what we put out. I liken it more to how we can change the filter we use to see things. Did you ever play the Punch-Buggy game as a kid? Whenever a Volkswagen beetle drove by, you'd get to punch the person next to you. It's a fun game, but the curious thing is while you drive down the road, you normally don't really notice many Volkswagen Beetles, but once you start to play the game and focus only on Beetles, you start to see a lot more of them. The universe works kind of in the same way.

If you're not focused and thankful, if you're not looking at the things that are good in your life, you lose them. They fade off beyond your field of vision. But once you start to recognize them and bring them back into your focus, you start to see more and more of the good stuff. It is a matter of flipping the switch; if you can figure out what you are thankful for, you can figure out what you should focus on.

My sons and I study American Kenpo Karate. In our class, the students are taught three rules of attention: focus your eyes, focus your mind, and focus your body. By studying these skills and practicing them, we found focus to be a big key in how we live our lives. What if you could have, be, or do whatever you wanted simply by focusing on it? What if the things you received in life were chosen by the thoughts you think?

What if you could choose what you wanted in life and just place an order to get it?

I have found that this works really well for my kids, too. If they're going on a rant about how bad things are, I have them focus on the good things in their life. From that they begin to identify more of the good things in their lives for which to be thankful.

Our first "switch flipping" happened on the second day of our family vacation. We had already driven six hours to a quiet Virginia town to rest and take a break. The next morning, we woke up bright eyed and bushy tailed ready to head off to Dollywood—another six hours away! The day started out less than perfect with a cold breakfast buffet, which should have been hot, and a long line at the malfunctioning microwave. We left all that behind in search of more appetizing options and stumbled upon a quaint cafe! Things were looking up—that is until the server left us standing for way too long only to forget half of our food and then serve my seven-year-old curdled milk! He had been begging for hot chocolate all morning anyway, so I guess that was a sign.

We were clearly caught up in whine and complain mode with little hope of escape unless one of us took action. That's where Mom the Dream Coach® stepped in. My husband had left the table to seek refuge in the men's room, so I announced to my two children that we would be flipping the switch and taking ourselves into "positive" mode starting now.

Unfortunately, because Chris was not present for the switch-flipping ritual, this left "Team Positive" one member short. Funny thing about that, though, it opened a tremendous door of opportunity to have a really great conversation, literally right down the road. It started with a comment about the weather.

"I was hoping it would be a nicer day," Chris grumbled.

"Why? So we could spend a beautiful day trapped in the car for six hours? I'd rather drive on a cloudy day and spend the nice ones outside. Positive thoughts, remember?" I reminded him.

"Positive thoughts can't change the weather," he assured me. He continued on with his hypothesis, "I think that's my problem with this whole manifestation thing; it promotes unrealistic thinking and impossible ideals and sets people up for false hope and disappointment."

"How's that?" I asked.

"It encourages people to believe they can accomplish the impossible just by thinking about it. It sets them up for disappointment. It's like standing them in front of a brick wall and telling them to wish to be on the other side. No matter how badly they want it, they cannot walk through a brick wall. It's impossible! But you tell them that if they want it badly enough they can. It's false hope, and at the end of the day, they are only disappointed that they failed. Here's the deal. I read the weather forecast. It's cloudy because of a storm system spanning three states. No amount of positive thinking can change that. Period."

I understood his thought process, but I kept thinking to myself, *Look for the positive here.*

"Chris, I guess the difference is that I appreciate that it's merely cloudy and not raining. I am thankful that we won't melt at the amusement park and the lines won't be as bad if negative people stay away because of the forecast. What I'm trying to say is that I do hear you, and I think I understand why you have trouble with manifestation. I think it's because you're looking at it all wrong. This concept isn't based on wishing and hoping for the impossible, it's about recognizing and appreciating the positive. I think that's why you feel many people wouldn't be open to it, because it's actually about reprogramming your brain and how you view the world.

"If all we focus on is the negative, then all we will see is the bad, the pain, and the sadness. We emphasize it and in a sense bring more of it to us through our own thoughts and focus. However, if we 'flip the switch' like the boys and I did at the restaurant, and focus on the positive and appreciate and acknowledge what we have, we see more of the good, happy, and positive. In essence, we are bringing more of the good to us. That's the basis of the Law of Attraction. It's not about creating false hope, but if we trust it and believe it, we start to expect miracles."

I had been spouting my opinion for a quite awhile, and by now I was beginning to notice that Chris wasn't interrupting, which was odd. Then I noticed the devilish grin creeping across his face, and about that same time, I began to feel warmth on my arm.

"You see it, don't you?" I asked slyly.

Chris was laughing, "So what?"

"The sun is shining, Chris! Even though you read the forecast and saw that cloud spanning three states, the sun is shining!"

We burst into laughter. It felt good!

That's the Law of Attraction.

If we stand in front of that brick wall and curse it for being there and getting in our way, all we will ever see is the brick wall. But if we choose to acknowledge its strength and appreciate that it's serving it's purpose and keeping us safe, perhaps ten paces down the wall we will find a ladder or a doorway to get us to the other side.

The more good we see in the world, the more good we receive in the world. Have you ever had someone tell you something cool about yourself that you hadn't thought of before, and all of a sudden you started to notice that great thing about you getting better and better? Have you ever thought about someone you haven't seen or talked to in awhile, and then suddenly they call you or you run into them somewhere? It's funny how that works, isn't it? It's kind of like you made the request and it was honored!

One of the first things we are taught to say as children is "thank you." We are instructed to be thankful for everything we receive in life by everyone who teaches us throughout life. I believe that the single most important thing we can say to anyone is, in fact, "Thank you!"

One way we make sure to bring good things into our lives is to give thanks everyday for the things we appreciate. So as you end each day, acknowledge the gifts you received. You can give thanks in a prayer or in your quiet time or in your journal. But no matter how you do it, do it faithfully each and every day. When you are honest and consistent, you will begin to see your daily gifts grow greater every day.

If you aren't sure what to give thanks for, ask your journal partner to go first and tell you what they are thankful for. You'll probably find that the most precious gifts are not toys or cars or material things. They are more like blessings: a warm bed, a full stomach, sight, laughter, the warmth of the sun, a loving person to read to you and tuck you in.

Probably the best gift of all is you! There's nothing wrong with being thankful for whatever brings you joy.

This world has programmed us to complain about anything we don't like or take offense to. It's a true, sad statistic that people will tell seven times more people about a negative experience than they will a positive one. The time is here to flip the switch. Start recognizing the good stuff. Turn on the charm and spread the wealth of a positive attitude. Punch buggy—no punch backs!

ACTIVITY: SMILE (SMALL MEMORIES INSPIRING LAUGHTER EVERYDAY) ALBUM

The smile album was inspired when I worked with Discovery Toys. I had a very large team of very fun people. They would send me cards and gifts, and when I did good things they were very generous with their gratitude and their congratulations. I was going through some really tough stuff at the time and would have entire days when I was completely down in the dumps and wouldn't even want to get out of bed. I found myself seeking out those things that would boost me up, those letters of congratulations. I lived for the the expressions that told me the company needed more people like me and that I had made someone believe in him or herself. Those notes made all the difference.

This gave me the idea to collect those things that made me happy and keep them in one place. I got one of those little photo albums and started collecting everything that made me smile—basically, small memories that inspired laughter every day. For example, I had a picture of my little sister Becky when she was really small. We had crimped her hair with one of those crimping irons, and she was wearing a rainbow dress. It was the goofiest looking picture, and it made me laugh hysterically every time I looked at it. I would include a joke of the day that somebody sent me by e-mail, or a picture in a magazine that made me laugh. Anything that raised my spirits went into that album.

I found that just by having one thing I could turn to when I was feeling down in the dumps, I could often change my direction for the entire rest of the day. I think it's really important that everybody have something like that. Everybody has those moments when they're appreciated and recognized, everybody has those things that bring them joy, and I think we need to focus on those things more.

Today, start your own smile album. Paste and copy into this book anything that makes you smile.

DAILY JOURNALING

Starting today, you will be writing at least three things that you are thankful for every day. Think of those things you would like to see more of in your life. If you start to think about the things you DON'T want, quickly turn those thoughts around by thinking of what you appreciate in your life. In other words, instead of writing: *I am thankful that I am not sick*, write down: *I am thankful that I am healthy.*

If you get to three things and you feel like writing more, GO AHEAD! You can never be too thankful. Still, try to make each day different because there are so many things in life to be thankful for!

*In difficult times, keep something beautiful in
your heart.* —JOHN O'DONOHUE

Day One: List three things that I am thankful for today.

_____

_____

_____

_____

_____

_____

_____

_____

_____

_____

_____

_____

_____

_____

_____

_____

_____

_____

_____

_____

*All that a man achieves and all that he fails to achieve are
the direct result of his own thoughts.* —JAMES ALLEN

Day Two: List three things I was thankful
for at school or at work today.

_____

_____

_____

_____

_____

_____

_____

_____

_____

_____

_____

_____

_____

_____

_____

_____

_____

_____

_____

_____

We may run, walk, stumble, drive, or fly, but let us never lose sight of the reason for the journey or miss a chance to see a rainbow on the way. —GLORIA GAITHER

Day Three: List three things I am thankful for in nature.

This bright new day, complete with 24 hours of opportunities, choices, and attitudes comes with a perfectly matched set of 1,440 minutes. This unique gift, this one day, cannot be exchanged, replaced, or refunded. Handle with care. Make the most of it. There is only one to a customer! —JOHN POWELL

Day Four: Did you notice any special gifts you received today?

_____

_____

_____

_____

_____

_____

_____

_____

_____

_____

_____

_____

_____

_____

_____

_____

_____

_____

_____

_____

In ordinary life we hardly realize that we receive a great deal more then we give, and that it is only with gratitude that life becomes rich. —DIETRICH BONHOEFFER

Day Five: Did I rediscover anything in my life that I had taken for granted?

_____

_____

_____

_____

_____

_____

_____

_____

_____

_____

_____

_____

_____

_____

_____

_____

_____

_____

_____

A strong positive mental attitude will create more miracles than any wonder drug. —Patricia Neal

Day Six: List three things I am thankful for in regards to my family.

_____

_____

_____

_____

_____

_____

_____

_____

_____

_____

_____

_____

_____

_____

_____

_____

_____

Seventh Day Success Story:

* What did I learn this week?

_____

_____

_____

_____

_____

** What were some really cool things that
happened when I practiced what I learned?*

_____

_____

_____

_____

_____

* What would I change?

_____

_____

_____

_____

* What would I never want to forget?

_____

_____

_____

_____

_____

Chapter 7

Dig Deep— When We Give We Receive

"Only a life lived in the service to others is worth living."

TARA'S TRUTH #7:
There is nothing wrong with spoiling your child,
as long as you use those moments to teach them
that getting is good, but giving is better.

LET THEM SPOIL

I am a true believer that when we give we receive. I also believe that my children were a gift to me. I never really could understand it when people, usually of the older generation, would say to me, "You're going to spoil that child!"

How? How exactly am I going to literally spoil my children? By celebrating them with gifts? By letting them have something they asked for? By treating them to the best life I can afford? How is that spoiling them?

Nevertheless, a spoiled brat was not an appealing image to me, so I tried to think about what I could give to my boys without causing them to rot. As it is with any human, my only reference came from my own memories. I recalled amazing holidays and birthdays. I had four sets of grandparents and fourteen sets of aunts and uncles complete with cousins. Looking back, I had some truly bountiful celebrations as a child.

Still, after the ribbons and wrapping paper faded, things weren't quite so bountiful in my home, materialistically, that is. I had a home, but not always heat; I had food, but not always three squares a day; I had clothing, but not always store bought and rarely new; I was usually the second or third owner. We had a pot to pee in, but rarely paper to wipe with. To this day, that is a joke in my house.

When I was ten years old, my mom decided it was time to start raising a second family with her new husband, so over the next seven years, I would have new brother Jesse and two darling sisters, Jillian and Becky. By the time the youngest was born, I was a senior in high school and was working two or three jobs because I had learned to love having money.

My first experiment in how to truly spoil a child was conducted on my three siblings. They were willing subjects and enjoyed me immensely. When I walked in the door on Christmas Eve, they would shout, "Santa's here!" I would be tackled at the knees every time I came to visit. I still wonder if they were really that happy to see me, or if they were just anticipating the gifts. The truth is that I tried my very best to spoil them rotten.

However, my sisters have become the most unpretentious, unspoiled people I know. I still try to spoil them because they are my first "babies," but they are far more concerned with giving back than they are with receiving. I think because I had such great success with this

first batch of "children," I decided to see what would happen if I did the same thing with my own kids. Only this time, I'd do one better—I'd celebrate them every day!

Max was the first guinea pig. He was the first grandchild, the first son, the first nephew, and the cutest little round-headed monkey you ever saw. This made things quite sweet for little Max. Max got whatever Max wanted! And it showed!

I think the big clue came on Max's second Christmas. We had visited so many houses and opened so many presents that when we finally arrived at my in-laws, Max sat on the floor in front of the pile of gifts, looked at my husband and me, and said, "No more, you open!" That was the year we put the "three toys, no excuses" rule into place.

Around that same time, I joined a home party plan selling educational toys. My family hated it because I took away all their fun; the boys thought every day was Christmas. They began to wait at the door after their morning snack for the "brown man" (the UPS guy, and luckily he has a sense of humor) to bring big boxes…life was good.

I've never been one to follow the status quo, so I soon ventured away from the "home party" thing and started selling my toys in bigger and better ways. I sold them to schools, daycares, special needs organizations, corporations and charities. The ones that hold a special place in my heart are with the Marine Toys for Tots programs. I attended several events through the years, which were hosted by their event coordinators and volunteers.

As the boys grew older, they would begin to attend these events with me. They got to help out in food pantries, at toy warehouses, and even got to go along on a few distributions. Besides the new toys we collected for Toys for Tots, the boys were tasked with going through their old toys as well. Anything they hadn't played with in the last six months would be packed up and taken to a place where the children don't have any toys to play with.

Max was appalled at the idea of a child without toys, so he decided that because his birthday is the week before Christmas, he would give some of his presents to children's charities. Alex wasn't so easy, he still liked all his stuff! That didn't last long, though. He came around when he was allowed to come to the decision in his own time, and I reminded him of the kids at the food pantry who came because they had no food. Shocked, he said, "You mean they don't have toys either?" I guess the thought of starving paled in comparison to doing without a train set.

This was the beginning of a truly beautiful giving spirit that my children carry to this day. Although this experience explains the giving part, the part that has the most impact is the receiving—and I don't mean material gifts. I think the true gift for me is that for my children giving is just part of what they do. They can see a need when it arises, and they can choose what and to whom they will give.

My first real proof of this came from my son Max. We were at the checkout of a store, and on the counter we saw one of those jars with a picture of a small, bald child wearing an oxygen mask. "Why does she look like that?" he asked me. I told him it was because she has a disease in her lungs that takes away her breath. "She can't breathe?" "That's right, Max. The money they collect is to help find a cure for her disease."

I could see him holding his breath as he reached deep in his jeans pockets. By now the cashier had stopped ringing up my purchases and was watching Max intently. He pulled out a handful of change, some candy wrappers, and a super bouncy ball, and dumped the whole stash in the jar, then plunged back into his pockets for more.

"What are you doing, honey?" I asked. Max was still holding his breath, and in his strained voice he said, "She needs this so much more than me, Mom!" Now the cashier and I were both in tears. "That's one pretty awesome kid you have there," she said to me. "You aren't kidding!" I gave my son the "in public" one armed hug and kissed him on the head. "You are pretty awesome, Max! I'm really proud of you."

Max started to breathe again, and he smiled from ear to ear. I don't think he was smiling because of what we said to him, although I'm sure it helped. I believe he was smiling because he knew that he had made a difference in the life of another person.

We have had many more "proud mommy moments" since then, and each one is a gift, but that day certainly solidified it for me. My children have always been acutely aware of the fact that there are people that do without. I did this quite on purpose. I want them to realize how much they have, but I also want them to realize that they can make a difference in the world just by giving what they can—even if it's giving of their time or talents.

Technically, my kids *are* spoiled. I mean, they have what they want. But I found that by allowing them to be part of the giving end and doing things for others, there's really no way that I can spoil them because they're so appreciative of what they have, and they're so acutely aware that there are people out there that don't have. And they're so willing to give of themselves that I don't believe that there's any way I can spoil them.

There is nothing wrong with giving in abundance to your children when you use those giving moments to teach them that getting is good but giving is better, because when we give we receive. If you teach that lesson every time you give something, then I say: Let 'em spoil!

ACTIVITY: LETTERS OF GRATITUDE

This week, take some time to sit down and write a letter of thanks for something someone did for you or someone else. Whether it is a family member, teacher, leader, co-worker, friend, or someone at a business you've recently visited. Tell them the things you appreciate about them. Be as free with your praise as you would with your concerns, and pay extra special attention to the reaction you get both from them and yourself.

Another thing you can do this week is to brainstorm some ideas of how you can help a person or organization in need. What is a gift, talent, or item you can share to make someone else's life better and make a difference? Is there someone whose life would be a little better by simply sharing the gift of your time and presence?

DAILY JOURNALING

Philanthropy derives from Ancient Greek. It means, "to love people." It is any activity intended to promote goodness or improve our quality of life. When we do or give freely to help another person it's called philanthropy.

James Keller said, "A candle loses nothing by lighting another candle." Can you imagine how great it would be if everyone in the world gave a little bit of whatever they could every day? I believe that would surely make this world a better place for everyone. Don't you? When we give of ourselves without any expectation, we open ourselves up to receive more in life. When we give, we feel better and are happier, and the people we help feel better and are happier, too! And as we have already learned, when we are happy and positive, we attract happy, positive people and things to our lives!

Now it's your turn to start changing the world. Each day, list at least three things you did for someone else that day. It could be something big like donating your unused clothing and toys to a shelter or charity, or something not as big but just as important, like helping to clean up after dinner without being asked. No matter what it is, choose something that you did strictly for someone else that made you both feel happy.

Congratulations! You are a philanthropist!

*We cannot hold a torch to light another's path without
brightening our own.* —Ben Sweetland

Day One: What is something I did for someone else today?

_____

_____

_____

_____

_____

_____

_____

_____

_____

_____

_____

_____

_____

_____

_____

_____

_____

_____

_____

_____

Give more than you think is necessary and you will get more than you think you deserve. —Tara Kennedy-Kline

Day Two: If I had all the money in the world I would _____.

_____

_____

_____

_____

_____

_____

_____

_____

_____

_____

_____

_____

_____

_____

_____

_____

_____

_____

_____

_____

Don't be reluctant to give of yourself generously. It is the mark of caring and compassion and personal greatness. —BRIAN TRACY

Day Three: What is something I can do or give to help someone else?

_____

_____

_____

_____

_____

_____

_____

_____

_____

_____

_____

_____

_____

_____

_____

_____

_____

_____

_____

Remember, there is no such thing as a small act of kindness. Every act creates a ripple with no logical end. —SCOTT ADAMS

Day Four: What act of generosity did I witness today?

_____

_____

_____

_____

_____

_____

_____

_____

_____

_____

_____

_____

_____

_____

_____

_____

_____

_____

_____

Value is in the doer, not the deed. —DENIS WAITLEY

Day Five: I will make a goal to do _____ good things tomorrow. Describe one.

_____

_____

_____

_____

_____

_____

_____

_____

_____

_____

_____

_____

_____

_____

_____

_____

_____

_____

There is no greater joy, nor greater reward than to make a fundamental difference in someone's life. —MARY ROSE McGEADY

Day Six: What was the greatest thing I did for someone this week?

_____

_____

_____

_____

_____

_____

_____

_____

_____

_____

_____

_____

_____

_____

_____

_____

_____

_____

Seventh Day Success Story:

* What did I learn this week?

_____

_____

_____

_____

_____

** What were some really cool things that
happened when I practiced what I learned?*

_____

_____

_____

_____

_____

* What would I change?

_____

_____

_____

_____

* What would I never want to forget?

_____

_____

_____

_____

_____

Chapter 8

Leave Love Notes— Twenty-five Things I Love about You

"Love is a better teacher than duty."

TARA'S TRUTH #8:
Sometimes the only thing a child needs from us to help them make a good choice is to know that they are loved unconditionally.

LOVE AND BULLIES

There was a time in my life when I hated my situation. I regretted my choice to start a new job, and I obsessed over every little thing I disliked about everyone in my life. I didn't like the people around me, and I became focused on how angry and frustrated they made me. I couldn't just walk away or dismiss them because they were far too close to me and far too integral in my day-to-day life.

The thing was, my negative thoughts weren't making these people more negative, but they *were* keeping them drawn to me! One night when I had had an exceptionally bad day, I was getting ready to write in my gratitude journal, but instead of writing the ten things I was most grateful for, I decided that I would write down ten things that I liked about one person who had really bugged me all day. As I began to try to think of ten things I admired about this person, I found it was really hard to do, so I pictured her sitting in front of me, and I pictured myself telling her the attributes I liked about her and things I appreciated about her. When I got to the tenth point, a curious thing happened. I kept writing! Each new thing I wrote made me think of another. When I could finally think of no more, I had twenty-seven things on my page! The other thing I had was the warmest, most peaceful sense of calm and appreciation for this person who had been such an irritant to me half an hour ago!

I tore that page out of my journal and kept it in my pocket. Every time she did something that thoroughly irritated me, I thought about something on that list that I appreciated about her. It immediately diffused the situation for me. Actually, it was pretty miraculous. I actually found myself empathizing with her more and more.

Coincidentally, a lot of the things that I wrote that I admired and appreciated about her were things that I also felt were strengths of mine. I found that I was able to understand where she was coming from a little bit better, and she didn't irritate me nearly as much.

Later, my son had a similar situation. He was having problems with a kid at school. This child was making fun of him, and it started to become a daily thing. There really is not much worse in a kid's life than a bully.

I could see the situation going nowhere good fast, so I said, "You know what, buddy? I need you to sit down and make a list of ten things that you like or admire about this kid." He said, "That's ridiculous. I can't even think of two."

So I sat down with him and said, "Okay, just give me one," and he gave me one. Then I said, "All right, give me another one." By the time we were done, he had a ton of things on this kid's list that he actually really liked and admired about him.

I told my son, "Now I need you to carry this list in your pocket, and the next time he's bugging you, I need you to just think about one of those things on your list that you admire or like about this kid. Then nod, smile, and walk away. I don't want the last thing you remember about him to be something negative. I want the last thing you remember about him to be positive, even if you planted it there yourself."

And the most amazing thing happened. This kid doesn't bug him at all anymore; he actually says hi to him. One time we saw him in the store while we were looking at dart guns; this kid and his mom came up and started talking to us about the dart gun he had. This went from a bullying situation to the kid coming up to us in a store and talking to us. It was simply a matter of my son closing his mouth, thinking something positive, and walking away.

This works in so many situations. Another time I was working with a youth services counselor, who was dealing with a situation in which a mother and her teenage daughter weren't getting along. The girl was being self-destructive, and it was just a really bad situation.

I suggested that the mom get a box and write down fifty things that she loved about her daughter, then tear them up into separate scraps of paper, and put them in the box. Every time the daughter had a negative thought about herself or her parent or whatever, she was supposed to open that box and take out one of those pieces of paper and read the thing that her mom loved about her. Two weeks later, they found that this thirteen-year-old girl was doing this every morning before she would go to school, and she was carrying this piece of paper with her in her pocket.

It made me realize that the twenty-five things you love about somebody don't just have to be words on a page; they can actually become talismans, a constant reminder that there are lovable things about them. This affirming ode might be what prevents someone from making a bad choice, or something worse.

This list has become a tremendous tool with my boys and my clients as well, and I have suggested using it in coaching and family counseling with tweens and teens. Every time I hear someone complaining incessantly about someone else, I tell them to make a list of things they like about that person and carry it with them to read anytime they feel they can't get past their own hurdles. Eventually, they will start to notice that person living up to the greatness they have labeled them with.

ACTIVITY: LOVE BOX

An activity to do either with or for someone you love is to make a treasure chest of "things I love about you." Imagine your naturally angry thirteen-year-old waking up each day and lifting the lid of their treasure chest, pulling out a random slip of paper, and opening it. On the paper is written, "I love to hear you sing in your room." It sounds ridiculous, but it's just one of the many things you love about your child…and to them, it means the world.

You will need:

- Some quiet time and a place to work

- A pad of paper

- A pen, pencil, or crayon

- Scissors

- An empty box (tissue boxes work really well, but you can get fancy if you'd like.)

- Decorations for your box

- An open mind and a loving heart

Sit down with your pad of paper and think about someone you want to "gift" your loving thoughts to. Write one thing you love about this person (or respect or admire...) on each line. When you have written at least twenty-five things, cut each line so that you have one sentiment on each strip of paper. (For instance, *I love the way you sing while you cook. I love the way you tie your shoes.*) Fold each strip to make a little box or package. Decorate your box with paper or stickers or whatever you'd like. Put the little bundles in the box. Write the instructions on a card or on the box.

This is a treasure chest for when you feel blue.

Reach in a grab one then here's what to do:

Open and read it and know that it's true.

Each treasure is something I love about you.

DAILY JOURNALING

I was blessed with two sets of parents for nearly all my life. But I didn't always see it that way. My parents divorced before I was two years old and by the time I was four they had formed new relationships with my stepparents. I realize now that I had the best of both worlds as a result, but at the time, I resented my stepparents immensely. I always believed they were trying to change me or control me and I made it very clear to them that they were NOT my parents. I remember on my tenth birthday, my step dad, Raymond with whom I had a particularly strained relationship, gave me a book (now that I recall, it was a journal!). In the front of the book he had written a message to me. It said, "Dear Tara, Happy Birthday to a wonderful girl. I have always loved you as if you were my own daughter. With Love, Raymond"

It was short and simple and took six years to say, but those words changed me that day, as well as the way I will look at him forever. From that moment, I loved him, too.

You may want to take this opportunity to share ten things you love about your journal partner and have them write down what you say, then have them do the same for you. It's amazing how much you are loved!

Kindness is more important than wisdom, and the recognition of this is the beginning of wisdom. —THEODORE ISAAC RUBIN

Day One: What does love mean to me?

_____

_____

_____

_____

_____

_____

_____

_____

_____

_____

_____

_____

_____

_____

_____

_____

_____

_____

_____

_____

When we seek to discover the best in others, we somehow bring out the best in ourselves. —WILLIAM ARTHUR WARD

Day Two: What are my favorite things about my best friend?

_____

_____

_____

_____

_____

_____

_____

_____

_____

_____

_____

_____

_____

_____

_____

_____

_____

_____

_____

_____

Life is made of memorable moments. We must teach ourselves to really live…to love the journey not the destination. —ANNA QUINDLEN

Day Three: What are five small things I noticed about my teacher, boss, or partner that made a huge and wonderful impact on my day today?

_____

_____

_____

_____

_____

_____

_____

_____

_____

_____

_____

_____

_____

_____

_____

_____

_____

_____

Every person ever created is so special that their presence in the world makes it richer and fuller and more wonderful than it could ever have been without them. —JOHN RUSKIN

Day Four: Think of someone doing a job, whether it is a soldier or a hairdresser. Write them a letter telling them what a great job they did.

_____

_____

_____

_____

_____

_____

_____

_____

_____

_____

_____

_____

_____

_____

_____

_____

_____

_____

_____

_____

Never look down on anybody, unless you are helping them up. —JESSE JACKSON

Day Five: Name someone who has bothered me lately. Ten things that I like or admire about him or her are _____.

_____

_____

_____

_____

_____

_____

_____

_____

_____

_____

_____

_____

_____

_____

_____

Did you stop at ten? How did you feel about that person when you were finished? Keep the list, and the next time you are feeling frustrated with that person, read it.

When you choose to be pleasant and positive in the way you treat others, you have also decided, in most cases, how you are going to be treated by others. —ZIG ZIGLAR

Day Six: What was something cool that happened when I approached a troubled relationship with a fresh perspective?

_____

_____

_____

_____

_____

_____

_____

_____

_____

_____

_____

_____

_____

_____

_____

_____

_____

_____

_____

Seventh Day Success Story:

* *What did I learn this week?*

_____

_____

_____

_____

_____

* *What were some really cool things that happened when I practiced what I learned?*

_____

_____

_____

_____

_____

* *What would I change?*

_____

_____

_____

_____

* *What would I never want to forget?*

_____

_____

_____

_____

_____

Chapter 9

See Beyond Your Beliefs— Live the Life You Dream

"Imagination is everything. It is the preview of life's coming attractions."

TARA'S TRUTH #9:
Every child should be allowed to dream. It comes naturally
to them, and as parents, we mustn't interfere. If children
learn through play, they grow through dreams.

DREAM DROPOUTS AND DAYDREAMERS

We are all children of the universe—and children dream wildly and dream big!

When I started my Dream Coaching®, I came to realize that as adults we have to be taught how to dream again. At some point in our life we forgot how. Kids dream crazy. Kids dream awesome! Where is this lost? In my dream world, it's never lost. I believe that kids should be left to be kids for a really long time. One of the greatest gifts that we can give our children is to allow and encourage them to dream for as long as they possibly can, if not forever.

One of my first public experiences with this occurred when my boys and I were standing in line for a roller coaster at an amusement park. As you now know, my son Alex plans to build a rollercoaster on the moon. He can draw it, describe it in detail, and tell you everything about it. While we were waiting in line, he was telling us about growing up to be an astronaut and building a roller coaster on the moon. My response to him, which was perfectly natural, was, "That'll be awesome. I can't wait to ride it."

When I looked around, several adults standing around us were looking at me like I was blowing spit bubbles, just because I was encouraging this child to believe in something so foolish as building a roller coaster on the moon. Can he do it? Today? *Of course not*, my realistic side says, but my dreamer says, *Why not?* If he believes in it strongly enough and can envision it, the Law of Attraction says he should have it. And even if he never gets to build that roller coaster, who's to say that the encouragement of being allowed to dream freely won't manifest into something just as creative but more "down to Earth," like a space-themed amusement park, or a career as an astronaut who might make a breakthrough in space travel?

The truth is, one day his dream may come true, but right now, today, he isn't ready. The beauty of the whole thing, however, is that if this is truly his dream and he walks the path of his life in pursuit of that dream, writes it down, researches it, studies it, and believes in it, by the time my little Alex is ready to realize his dream twenty or thirty years from now, we may very well have an amusement park on the moon, and my son will have surely designed their rollercoaster!

As far as our spirit and our joy and our fun, we lose a lot as adults. It's as if somewhere along the line someone told us that it was no longer okay to dream. And from that point on, we grounded ourselves in reality to the level that we never allowed ourselves to grow further. I believe that we grow through our dreams. There's a phenomenon called apoptosis, which is the breakdown or "death" of cells once they have outlived their purpose. There are studies that have shown that the introduction of endorphins and new goals and dreams in individuals shown to be in this state of deterioration has actually slowed the cell death process and in some cases has introduced new, healthy cell growth.

Using this information, it's very possible to believe that people who continue to dream and strive towards their dreams live longer, healthier, happier lives than those who are grounded in their doubt and believe they have outlived their purpose.

Many of us stop dreaming because we are frustrated by the length of time it takes for our dreams to come true. When that happens we become what I call "dream dropouts." The thing is, it's not so much the achieving of the dream as it is who we become along the path to achieving that dream that makes us great.

What we are experiencing in these "temper tantrums of faith" is that perhaps we aren't doing enough to personally and spiritually grow into our dreams. It is often said, "When the student is ready, the teacher will appear." If that is the case, then it could be that in those times when we are feeling impatient and fed up, it isn't necessarily that our dream is too big but rather that our belief is too small. We simply are not ready yet.

When we dream, we are basically telling ourselves that we believe in our own abilities and we want to achieve the greatest "self" we are capable of. Some people believe that it is selfish to dream. I believe that we cannot truly find ourselves unless we dream!

Our dreams can allow and even teach us to be extremely generous. The more we fill our lives with passion and abundance through our dreams, the more we will have to share and give to others. I've been criticized for dreaming of becoming a millionaire, to which I've often said, "If I want to donate a million dollars to charity, I must first acquire a million dollars!" Does that make me selfish for dreaming of being a millionaire?

As we achieve our own dreams, we develop the ability to help others achieve their dreams, too. Imagine what a beautiful world that would be!

You may already have a dream that you've been keeping to yourself. You may just be realizing that it's okay to have a dream, or you may feel that dreaming isn't your thing. Regardless, I would challenge you to spend one week thinking with the imagination and spirit of a child! Learn how to re-create your dream.

Most of us spend a lot of time daydreaming, but many of us stop ourselves short when we either catch ourselves or are caught in the process. Whether out of guilt or because of something we were told or taught (*Keep your head out of the clouds.* or *Be realistic!*), most of us think small. But if you've ever noticed the joy and delight of a child playing make-believe, you know that magic exists. Children don't know our "adult limits." They believe anything is possible, and the simple act of imagining the impossible makes life more enjoyable.

I want to encourage you to take some time to let yourself imagine the possibilities of your life. Don't just think about what is realistic. Consider what might seem nearly outrageous about what would require you to grow and move beyond who it is you currently know yourself to be. Think about what you have always wanted to do, be, or have in your life, and listen carefully to those things that come to you in your thoughts and dreams.

My favorite quote from a song is from Michael Jackson's "Man in the Mirror." It goes, "If you want to make the world a better place, take a look at yourself, and then make that change." If you want change in your life, it's up to you! When you want something you've never had, you've got to do something you've never done. You decide. You get to choose your thoughts. Try giving big thought and energy to the direction of your life and who you want to be as a spouse, parent, and person. Create your own success story!

During this process, I am going to ask you to think outside the box. That might mean owning an island in the South Pacific, or it might be a more loving, stress-free relationship with your family. Whatever it is, don't hold back! Be outrageous and let your imagination fly. This does not mean thinking unrealistic, pie-in-the-sky stuff, like being able to fly or grow six inches in a day; it simply means allowing yourself to stretch and believe in the possibility of your dreams.

ACTIVITY: VISION BOARD

This is one of the coolest activities we do together as a family because it lets us explore together, the beauty of our dreams!

Besides a large area to work, an open mind, and a playful spirit, you will need:

- Poster board, display board, cork board

- Pencils, markers, crayons, paint, etc.

- Pictures, words, phrases, quotes—anything that inspires you to think about your dreams

- Glue or tape

First divide your poster into four sections: My Dreams for What I Want to Do, Be, Give and Have. Cut out pictures and words that remind you of your dream goals and then place those cutouts on your poster in one of the four sections.

For example, under What I Want to Do, I have pictures of places I want to vacation, trips I have taken with my kids, and the words "Dream & Travel," to name a few. Under What I Want to Be, I have pictures of my mentors, both spiritual and professional, a mock-up of my speaker ad as well as a PhotoShopped picture of my head on my dream body. Under What I Want to Have are pictures of my dream yard, my dream car, and my friends, and under What I Want to Give, I have Monopoly money, pictures of baskets of food, toys, and medication next to the names and logos of the charities I support.

Have fun with this project, and whatever you do—dream big! Because really, what's the worst thing that could happen if you achieved everything you dreamed of? Remember: It's not the size of the dream but the effort you put into achieving it that makes you great!

DAILY JOURNALING

This week, I want you and your children to pretend that you are watching a movie in which you are the star. Close your eyes and see each dream being played out in 4-D. See each place, person, and action in full color. Hear the sounds, feel the breezes, taste the flavors, and experience the emotions of everything around you.

For the next few days, open your mind and share what happens in the screen adaption of your perfect life.

Dreams come true; without that possibility, nature would not incite us to have them. —JOHN UPDIKE

Day One: What does my perfect day look like?

It's not what you know but what you believe that determines your success in life. —TARA KENNEDY-KLINE

Day Two: What will I be when I grow up?

_____

_____

_____

_____

_____

_____

_____

_____

_____

_____

_____

_____

_____

_____

_____

_____

_____

_____

_____

All men dream but not equally. Those who dream by night in the dusty recesses of their minds wake in the day to find that it was vanity; but the dreamers of the day are dangerous men, for they may act their dream with open eyes to make it possible. —T.E. LAWRENCE

Day Three: If there were no limits (like time, money or support of my family and friends) , what would I do?

_____

_____

_____

_____

_____

_____

_____

_____

_____

_____

_____

_____

_____

_____

_____

_____

_____

_____

_____

Cherish your visions and your dreams, as they are the children of your soul, the blueprints of your ultimate achievements. —NAPOLEON HILL

Day Four: What do I dream for me?

_____

_____

_____

_____

_____

_____

_____

_____

_____

_____

_____

_____

_____

_____

_____

_____

_____

_____

_____

_____

We dream so we don't have to be apart so long. If we're in each other's dreams, we can play together all night. —BILL WATTERSON

Day Five: My dream for you, my journal buddy, is _____.

_____

_____

_____

_____

_____

_____

_____

_____

_____

_____

_____

_____

_____

_____

_____

_____

_____

_____

_____

The future belongs to those who believe in the beauty of their dreams. —ELEANOR ROOSEVELT

Day Six: What does my perfect world look like?

_____

_____

_____

_____

_____

_____

_____

_____

_____

_____

_____

_____

_____

_____

_____

_____

_____

_____

_____

_____

Seventh Day Success Story:

* *What did I learn this week?*

_____

_____

_____

_____

_____

* *What were some really cool things that
happened when I practiced what I learned?*

_____

_____

_____

_____

_____

* *What would I change?*

_____

_____

_____

_____

* *What would I never want to forget?*

_____

_____

_____

_____

_____

Chapter 10

Surround Yourself with Light— Raising Your Attitude Average

"Most people say that it is the intellect which makes a great scientist. They are wrong: it is character."

TARA'S TRUTH #10:
We need to be aware of who we are becoming and what we are creating based on the people we surround ourselves with—and we must be willing to adjust this when necessary.

BLESS AND RELEASE

One of the things that I found to be extremely beneficial with my kids was the concept that we're the average of the five people we spend the most time with. It is all up to us. We either become or create the average attitude of the people we spend the most time with.

This one really landed with me in a big way when I was going through depression. When I took a look around at the people I was spending the most time with, I realized that they were actually feeding my depression. I was surrounding myself with people that were depressed about their own lives. All they did was complain about this or that.

If I told them something that had gone wrong, they would commiserate with me, but they never boosted me up. I didn't have anyone taking me by the hand and pulling me out of it. I was surrounding myself with people that were digging the hole deeper with me.

When I agreed to seek out other, positive people to spend my time with, my life changed. I think that's probably also why my coming out of my depression is coincident with moving; we moved to an area that is so positive, friendly, and embracing that I found myself surrounded by people who were joyful. It completely changed who I was and the way I thought about things.

I remember we moved there right at the end of the school year. Many of the parents go to the school's playground to pick up their kids, and they congregate there before school is out. Eventually, I finally started getting into conversations with some of the moms. One day I said, "Oh, my gosh. My boys are going to be out of school soon. Then I'm going to have them all day long." One mom looked at me and said, "I can't wait for my kids to get out of school. I love having them at home with me."

It caught me off guard that someone could actually be that positive and excited. At the same time, I was a little bit offended. Then I thought to myself, *This is one of the people I want to spend the most time with, because that's where I want to be some day.* Now she's one of my closest friends. The thing that was really cool is that as I started spending more time with these positive people, it started to change the dynamics of who I was. When I went back to my other friends, I was actually the person who raised the average for them.

Now, these friends that I've gotten back in contact with come to me if they're feeling down, and they look to me to bring them up. We don't commiserate anymore. We talk about the great stories that celebrate our families and celebrate us. By doing that, we're raising the average.

Max had a friend who was a pretty negative kid, the sort of kid who hates school and "everything sucks," which is language kids don't use in our house. This kid was always using such language and doing and saying things that aren't in sync with who we are as a family.

One day during our journaling, I asked Max to tell me who his best friends were. He rattled off a few and, of course, this child was one of them. I said, "Tell me a little bit more about him and how you see him as a person." He told me how negative his friend was. I said, "So, would you want people to look at you and describe you in the same way that they describe your friend?" He said, "No way." I replied, "Well, the more time you spend with this person, the more you're going to start to be like him. That concerns me."

I continued, "You do have a choice here. You can choose to bless and release him. You don't have to say that you don't want to be friends with him anymore, but you don't have to spend so much time with him either, and you could seek out some other kids that you do want to spend more time with." Now, I admit that was probably the wrong way for me to go at the time, but as it turned out, Max flipped it. He said, "Or maybe by him spending more time with me, I could just change him," which I thought was a really good idea.

This topic is normally very controversial. We tend to say to our kids, "I don't want you to hang around that person anymore, because I don't like them." But instead of saying, "I don't want you to see this person anymore," we can say to them, "Are those traits that we want people to see in you?" By letting our children make those choices on their own, and either spend less time with the kid or decide to make it their mission to change that kid, we empower them. We get better results out of introducing it in such a way that our kids can contemplate it for themselves than by forcing alienation, which ultimately forces rebellion.

When there are times that we need to completely change the company we keep, it becomes a matter of blessing and releasing those people. At the end of the day, it is imperative that we create our own circle of excellence.

DAILY JOURNALING

This week while you are journaling, consider what you would want to hear people saying about you if you were standing right outside their door. When you talk about the people you admire, do they have those same traits and gifts?

As my hero Jack Canfield says: Are you the kind of person who lights up a room when you walk in or when you walk out?

Trust men and they will be true to you; treat them greatly and they will show themselves great. —RALPH WALDO EMERSON

Day One: My five heroes are _____.
They're my heroes because _____.

_____

_____

_____

_____

_____

_____

_____

_____

_____

_____

_____

_____

_____

_____

_____

_____

_____

_____

If we want our children to possess the traits of character we most admire, we need to teach them what those traits are and why they deserve both admiration and allegiance. —WILLIAM J. BENNETT

Day Two: My best friends are _____. What I like best about them is _____.

_____

_____

_____

_____

_____

_____

_____

_____

_____

_____

_____

_____

_____

_____

_____

_____

_____

_____

_____

Keep away from people who try to belittle your ambitions.
Small people always do that, but the really great make you
feel that you too can become great. —MARK TWAIN

Day Three: If I could choose five people to take on an adventure, who would they be?

_____

_____

_____

_____

_____

_____

_____

_____

_____

_____

_____

_____

_____

_____

_____

_____

_____

_____

The best index to a person's character is (a) how he treats people who can't do him any good, and (b) how he treats people who can't fight back. —ABIGAIL VAN BUREN

Day Four: The five most important people on the planet are _____.

_____

_____

_____

_____

_____

_____

_____

_____

_____

_____

_____

_____

_____

_____

_____

_____

_____

_____

_____

We judge ourselves by what we feel capable of doing, while others judge us by what we have already done. —HENRY WADSWORTH LONGFELLOW

Day Five: Who is someone I see every day but don't know anything about? What are five questions I would like to ask them?

_____

_____

_____

_____

_____

_____

_____

_____

_____

_____

_____

_____

_____

_____

_____

_____

_____

_____

_____

_____

The question for the child is not do I want to be good? But whom do I want to be like? —BRUNO BETTELHEIM

Day Six: I would love to spend more time with _____.

_____

_____

_____

_____

_____

_____

_____

_____

_____

_____

_____

_____

_____

_____

_____

_____

_____

_____

_____

_____

Seventh Day Success Story:

* *What did I learn this week?*

_____

_____

_____

_____

_____

* *What were some really cool things that
happened when I practiced what I learned?*

_____

_____

_____

_____

_____

* *What would I change?*

_____

_____

_____

_____

* *What would I never want to forget?*

_____

_____

_____

_____

_____

Chapter 11

Give Them a Dark Hall to Run Down— Creating Your Quiet Space

"Not everything that can be counted counts, and not everything that counts can be counted."

TARA'S TRUTH #11:
Time out should be for both the child and the caretaker. It is more important that it be a space to regroup and decompress than punish the child.

TIME OUT IS FOR BOTH OF YOU

Once my husband and I took my son Alex to a wrestling match to watch his brother Max. We walked into this strange school gymnasium and could hear the sounds of people shouting and cheering. It was so loud, and the lights were glaring. It completely freaked Alex out. He tore away from me and ran down a dark hallway in this unfamiliar school.

I started running after him, and when I got about halfway down the hallway, I realized Alex was standing at a gate in the middle of the hallway. He couldn't get any further. I stopped, too, and thought to myself, *I've got two choices here. I can either go down there and grab him and drag him out kicking and screaming and force him into a horrible situation. Or I can stop for a minute and think about this.*

I stopped and sat down. Then I said, "Hey, buddy. What's going on?"

He answered, "It's too loud in there. There are too many lights. I don't want to go in there."

I said, "I understand. It's kind of scary, but you know, you can't tear away from me again because that scared me." We talked about what could happen, and agreed that I would walk him into the gymnasium, and if he got too scared, we would walk out.

So Alex came out to me on his own when he was ready and when he felt comfortable. If I had dragged him out, I would have accomplished nothing. He probably would have taken off again, or he would have started ranting and raving and screaming and yelling. By giving him the opportunity in that hallway to take the time to cool down and compose himself, and do a reality check and see that it wasn't quite as bad as he thought, we were able to make it through the entire wrestling match without incident.

I realized that there had been a lot of times when one of my boys would have a meltdown or start yelling and screaming about something, and I would instinctively start yelling and screaming back to defend myself. In reality, what we both needed to do was separate ourselves from each other and give each other a time out. The whole premise that "time out is for both of you" comes from this.

I believe that the silliest thing we can do to our child is to sit them in a chair and say, "Think about what you did wrong for fifteen minutes."

In reality, in those situations where we're fighting with our own child, what we both need is a break from each other.

In our family, it's not "sit in a chair and think about it." It's "go take a break for awhile." Alex can go to his room and play with his Legos, draw on his chalkboard, whatever he wants to do in that room, short of destroying it, for ten minutes. I do the same thing, because in those moments when things get inflamed and ugly, I need the break just as much as he does. A lot of times when we lash out, it's because we're having our own temper tantrum, or one of us is tired. If we get that time away from each other to decompress, it really works.

The thing that's so funny is the technique has also worked for Alex in school. When I told his teacher about this, she gave him a timer, and when he felt like he was losing control in the classroom, she would set it for a minute. Alex would take it out into the hallway and decompress there for a minute. When the timer went off, he came back in the room and was able to integrate back into the class. It is a really awesome tool for him.

I think the thing that I love most about Alex's room is that we've created his quiet space. If we're at the grocery store where there is no dark hallway to run down, no quiet space to go to, I say to Alex, "I need you to come to attention right now. I need you to focus."

It goes back to the value of Kenpo marital arts training, I discussed in Chapter 6. Learning the attention stance and the two rules of attention, which are concentration and self-control has been invaluable. It is an amazing tool for kids to bring themselves into attention, concentration, and focus their minds. Because of Alex's training, he's able to do that in public places. I notice some people may look kind of funny at us, but he literally will stand at attention and focus himself. In that moment of concentration, he can center himself and calm himself down. I think that was the best gift that we could have given him, the ability to center himself.

Cast out the day is another concept they teach in Kenpo class. All the kids are in their attention stance at the beginning of class, and they are told to cast out the day. They all go into "horse stance," close their eyes, focus on recalling all the things that happened in their day, and then they release the whole day so they can be totally present for their class. It's really like a mini form of meditation.

Teaching our children to be present provides them with an invaluable skill. It can be something as simple as being present when the teacher is talking so they can learn. It enables kids to quiet themselves, too. There was a time when they had to put rubber bands around the base of Alex's chair so he had something to do with his feet because he was so fidgety and couldn't keep himself still. Now, he's able to close his eyes and "cast out his day," so that he won't have so much distraction in his head.

Every single child, whether they are on the spectrum or not, needs to be able to run down a dark hallway. Every single child needs to be able to learn the skills to calm themselves, to quiet their minds. Every single child needs to be given the opportunity to get a break from the situation they're in *before* we discipline them.

By definition, discipline is teaching by leading; but in today's society, it has become more of a reaction than a guide. When we discipline from a place of anger in order to get an immediate response, we're not teaching children anything. By recognizing that the problem may be just as much with us as it is with our kid, and recognizing that we need to give ourselves a break from each other, we are leading and teaching our children valuable skills like patience and self-control that are going to take us so much further than reaction. Ultimately, it's a type of strengthening.

ACTIVITY: CREATE YOUR FOCUS SPACE

I have realized that when tempers flare in my house, it's usually because someone is either hungry, frustrated, or needs a nap, so they are throwing a tantrum—and it's not always the kids! For that reason, I believe that time out should be the discipline of choice, and it should be *for adults and children*!

When I am ready to lose my temper with my kids, I will typically say something like this: "It's obvious we need a break from each other. Everyone to their rooms for ten minutes." I started timing by age, one minute for every year, but eventually they began to fight over that, too, so now it's ten minutes because that's easy.

After the ten minutes (or thirty minutes if you're doing this with your spouse) is up, we don't talk about the problem again unless we need to clear something up in order to be present for each other. We also make it very clear that if we do need to discuss an issue, the conversation must be positive and productive. If not, we "put it in a bubble and blow it away." The end.

This process has worked really well for us because (a) we stick to it, and (b) we have created a space for ourselves that allows us to relax and do what we love. The boys have their music, art materials, pets, and books in their rooms because that's their space to spend their "quiet time." I have also found that it is much easier for them to fall asleep at night because they have chosen to keep in their rooms the things that quiet their minds.

My space has a comfy chair, my favorite books, my exercise equipment, and my CD player as well as candles and chocolate—and yes, I do have a wine rack in there. Creating these spaces and using them faithfully has been a real blessing to our family. It's taught us how to decompress before we blow and has served to help us avoid many, many situations that could have led to bad choices and regrettable behavior.

If you feel you need to use a time out chair, make sure it's a cozy one in a quiet place away from the rest of hustle and bustle of your home and have each of your family members do the same.

DAILY JOURNALING

One of my teachers Arthur Joseph, who is the founder of the Vocal Awareness Institute, taught me the skill of "allowing a deep loving breath." I think that one of the most relaxing and calming things I have ever done is to simply learn how to breathe.

Take a deep breath. Did you feel you're your neck tighten and hear the noise the air made when you breathed in? Now close your eyes and think the words "I love you" while you "allow" the next breath. Notice the difference?

I call this relaxed breathing and you should practice it in your quiet time. In addition, find something positive or funny that you can focus on in the time it takes to breathe. Can you see how you can use these techniques to change your mood in a single breath?

Each day, take time to quiet your mind and focus on the events of your day. Picture it as if it had gone perfectly for you. Think of something that left you feeling confused or stuck and then in your quiet time, ask for guidance on how you can solve that problem as your greatest self. Focus on your breathing. When you are ready, open your eyes and share your thoughts with your journal partner.

Take your quiet time before you journal today. Write whatever comes into your mind when you open your eyes.

Happiness isn't something that depends on our surroundings. It's something we make inside ourselves. —CORRIE TEN BOOM

Day One: Where do I feel safe?

_____

_____

_____

_____

_____

_____

_____

_____

_____

_____

_____

_____

_____

_____

_____

_____

_____

_____

_____

_____

*If we are to reach real peace in this world…we shall
have to begin with the children.* —GANDHI

Day Two: When I am angry, I would like it if I could _____.

To the mind that is still, the whole Universe surrenders. —LAO TZU

Day Three: The best way for me to calm down is _____.

_____

_____

_____

_____

_____

_____

_____

_____

_____

_____

_____

_____

_____

_____

_____

_____

_____

_____

_____

No problem can be solved from the same level of consciousness that created it. —ALBERT EINSTEIN

Day Four: If I am in trouble, what is my biggest fear?

_____

_____

_____

_____

_____

_____

_____

_____

_____

_____

_____

_____

_____

_____

_____

_____

_____

_____

_____

_____

No one has yet fully realized the wealth of sympathy, kindness, and generosity hidden in the soul of a child. The effort of every true education should be to unlock that treasure. —EMMA GOLDMAN

Day Five: What is it that frustrates me the most in life?

_____

_____

_____

_____

_____

_____

_____

_____

_____

_____

_____

_____

_____

_____

_____

_____

_____

_____

_____

Imagination was given to us to compensate for what we are not; a sense of humor was given to us to console us for what we are. —Mack McGinnis

Day Six: Something you could say or do to help me focus is _____.

_____

_____

_____

_____

_____

_____

_____

_____

_____

_____

_____

_____

_____

_____

_____

_____

_____

_____

_____

_____

Seventh Day Success Story:

* *What did I learn this week?*

_____

_____

_____

_____

_____

* *What were some really cool things that
happened when I practiced what I learned?*

_____

_____

_____

_____

_____

* *What would I change?*

_____

_____

_____

_____

_____

* *What would I never want to forget?*

_____

_____

_____

_____

_____

Chapter 12

That Was Then, This Is Now— Resolve and Resolutions

"The only source of knowledge is experience."

TARA'S TRUTH #12:

It's easy to make promises to our children if we believe they will never remember what we said, but the truth is, children never truly forget. And those promises, whether kept or broken, will determine the integrity with which they live their lives.

UP, UP, AND AWAY: DO YOU WANT TO SAVE THE CHANGES YOU HAVE MADE?

I f you've ever written a paper or done any kind of work on a computer, you know that when you get ready to close the program the computer throws you a pretty serious reminder. It asks you, "Do you want to save the changes you have made?"

Now that you have come to the end of this program and have hopefully made some pretty significant amendments to your life, you have a choice to make. I am going to ask you to make an agreement—not with me, but with yourself and your journal partner. It would be so much easier to maintain the status quo, but instead, will you agree to "save the changes you have made" and continue to live a life of respect, integrity, intention, purpose, and dreams?

If so, let me be the first to thank you, because you are among the dreamers and are bound to make a difference in the world.

It's easy when things are romantic and we're in a honeymoon period to make that commitment and say, "This is what I'm going to do for the rest of my life." What's difficult is following through to make the changes you've made a part of your life and who you are.

I've stopped making New Year's resolutions because I've realized that I should be making resolutions constantly, not just one day a year. What I found during the journaling process with my kids was that I set little resolutions frequently. These were things that were so vital and so important to my family and the way that we move forward that failure was not an option. It is something that I've been doing for an entire year.

If this three-month journaling journey has made a change in your life, if you've seen a difference in the way you play with your children, the way you talk to them, and the way you have respect for each other, then make that commitment to make it a part of each day. The best way to do this is to take a look at where you were when you started. See how far you've come, and decide to make it a journey forward rather than a step back. Once you've got that momentum, it's a lot easier to keep moving in the right direction.

My little Alex taught me a beautiful lesson on how he sees me just recently. We were driving in the car and I was telling my husband about a mistake I made due to being scattered. I told him that "organization was my weakness." From the back of the car we heard Alex pipe up

"Hey Mom! That must mean you're a Super Hero because only Super heros have weaknesses!" My husband laughed and said THAT's going in the book! But the truth is, we were really laughing at the irony of it all. There was a time when I would take mistakes and failures, even my children's failures, and put them back on myself. I had gotten into the habit of not allowing myself to see my own successes, achievements, intelligence, and greatness. It was through listening to my children describe how they see me, and the cool things they see *in* me, that made all the difference. They think I am a hero, and you know what? I am. They see my husband as a hero, too. And I can vouch for that.

As parents we lose sight of how great we are, but in the end it's up, up, and away. Each of us must learn how to fly, to use our secret weapons and wonder powers if we want to make a difference in our children's lives and in the world. You have a choice to make. You can either keep doing the things that you've learned don't work, or you can use the tools you've learned to make family communication and self-awareness meaningful elements in your day-to-day living.

How has journaling changed you? How are you a better person? What have you learned about your journal buddy? What does your life look like a year from now?

My hope is that you've realized through the course of this process that it's not just your kids who can dream. It's not just your kids who can change their path. Hopefully you realize that regardless of how old you are, where you've been, or what you're doing in life, *you have the power to make changes within yourself.* By becoming that person, you're guiding your child in a way neither of you ever thought you would go, and the sky is the limit. Now that you've seen the greatness of your child and you, Stop raising Einstein—start celebrating the unique brilliance each of us offers.

DAILY JOURNALING

You have spent the last eleven weeks exploring new concepts and ideas and realizing the uniqueness that is you. Spend this next week reflecting on what you have learned as well as preparing for what you would like your life to become as you venture on as a Brilliant Dreamer.

Learn from yesterday, live for today, hope for tomorrow. The important thing is not to stop questioning. —ALBERT EINSTEIN

Day One: How has keeping a journal changed how I approach life?

_____

_____

_____

_____

_____

_____

_____

_____

_____

_____

_____

_____

_____

_____

_____

_____

_____

_____

_____

If there is anything we wish to change in the child, we should first examine it and see whether it is not something that could better be changed in ourselves. —CARL JUNG

Day Two: What have I learned about my journal buddy that I didn't know three months ago?

Ideals are like stars; you will not succeed in touching them with your hands. But like the seafaring man on the desert of waters, you choose them as your guides, and following them you will reach your destiny. —CARL SCHURZ

Day Three: What does my life look like a year from now?

_____

_____

_____

_____

_____

_____

_____

_____

_____

_____

_____

_____

_____

_____

_____

_____

_____

_____

_____

_____

Be happy. Talk happiness. Happiness calls out responsive gladness in others. There is enough sadness in the world without yours…never doubt the excellence and permanence of what is yet to be. Join the great company of those who make the barren places of life fruitful with kindness. Your success and happiness lie in you…the great enduring realities are love and service…resolve to keep happy and your joy and you shall form an invincible host against difficulties. —HELEN KELLER

Day Four: Tell a story that celebrates you.

_____

_____

_____

_____

_____

_____

_____

_____

_____

_____

_____

_____

_____

_____

_____

_____

_____

Don't let the fear of striking out keep you from playing the game.

Day Five: Free reign, tell a story that you want to share.

_____

_____

_____

_____

_____

_____

_____

_____

_____

_____

_____

_____

_____

_____

_____

_____

_____

_____

_____

With our thoughts we make the world. —BUDDHA

Day Six: How do you plan to make a difference in the world?

_____

_____

_____

_____

_____

_____

_____

_____

_____

_____

_____

_____

_____

_____

_____

_____

_____

_____

_____

_____

Seventh Day Success Story:

* *What did I learn this week?*

_____

_____

_____

_____

_____

* *What were some really cool things that happened when I practiced what I learned?*

_____

_____

_____

_____

_____

* *What would I change?*

_____

_____

_____

_____

* *What would I never want to forget?*

_____

_____

_____

_____

_____

Mahatma Gandhi said, "Be the change you want to see in the world."

For over a year I have kept a journal with both of my sons. Though each boy has his own style and practices, this process has absolutely transformed our lives.

The most substantial breakthrough we experienced was that Alex's IEP and OT were removed from his curriculum. Chris and I were thrilled. "That's AMAZING!" was my literal response. The teachers all agreed, but quickly noted that they had done nothing differently, so it must be something we were doing at home. I wracked my brain at the time and then finally figured out that it was the lessons, the communication, and the journaling that had made the difference for little Alex.

I began to really take a look at what had been happening in my life. What I saw that is truly remarkable to me is that I went from being a bankrupt, depressed, overwhelmed, overworked, and underappreciated person to being a successful business owner and a joyous and playful wife and mother.

Through journaling, I've realized that I could spend the rest of my life being sad about all the things that happened to me, or I could spend the rest of my life pursuing my dreams, giving thanks for those people and things that I do have in my life, and making the best life for my children.

I now see the gifts in me. I see the gifts in my spouse, and I see the gifts in my children.

Somewhere along the line I remembered those days when I was so desperately seeking a solution that didn't involve drugs or medicine and I realized that like Dorothy in the Land of Oz, the answer was right there with me all the while. It was truly a case of communication rather than medication for Alex and me. We created a new pattern of behavior, and it's a positive one.

Now, although there have been monumental changes, my life certainly isn't perfect. I can't say that we don't ever struggle or disagree. We don't always make the right choices. And sometimes it's not easy to see the gifts in the mistakes we make right away. But what I can say is that we have developed a relationship where we can address our choices and blunders with grace and sensibility and we can resolve them with love, communication, and compassion. We honor and respect one another as well as our promises. And I think most importantly, each of us is able to look at the world, each other, and ourselves to see the Unique Brilliance in it all.

 A Berks County, Pennsylvania, native, Tara Kennedy Kline is an Allentown Parenting Examiner, a certified Dream Coach®, and the owner of Tara's Toy Box™, a toy wholesaler dedicated to serving and supporting charitable and philanthropic programs.

In her late 30s, Tara was diagnosed with ADD. She struggled with anxiety, depression and loss—her brother died of a heart attack at 19 and her mother fell victim to leukemia at age 57. Finally, when she discovered her son had Asperger's Syndrome, her life turned around.

In a process that gave the title to this book, she learned how to communicate with him—then wrote a book to communicate what she had learned. In her own words, "This process saved my family, it saved my marriage and it saved my life. Now I want to give that same opportunity to everyone I touch. One conversation at a time."

Today, Tara lives in Pennsylvania with her two sons and her husband, Chris, who was her high school sweetheart.

For more information on speaking, coaching and workshops, please visit tarakennedykline.com

Printed in the USA
CPSIA information can be obtained
at www.ICGtesting.com
JSHW012032140824
68134JS00033B/3007